RICHARD PORTER AND I...

THE HAND OF CIRCUMSTANCE

ANGELA SOLOMON

TABLE OF CONTENTS

A Harlem Story

I grew up in Harlem, on the rough side of the street. My siblings and I were placed in foster care when I was about five, my mother died when I was 12, and I lost my virginity to a stranger when I was 12 going on 13. When I was 14, I hit the streets—running away—from place-to-place, home-to-home. I met Richard when I was 16, I had our daughter at 19, and before I turned 21, Richard was gone, and I had to make it on my own.

"Life is a game." We hear that all the time. And it really is. It's like a deck of cards. The cards are the circumstances, and we are all dealt our hand. Sometimes, you are dealt a good hand, and sometimes you are dealt a bad hand. And guess what? The dealers are your parents, like it or not. I understand they were probably dealt their own hand. I get it, but I also understood the game was in my hand and it was up to me to change it.

Richard and I were both dealt a hand that was very similar, the common denominator was the fact that both of our mothers were substance users . I'm not really sure why my parents used heroin and I definitely can't say why Richard's mother was a substance users. I don't judge. But I do know that because our parents were on drugsr it left us at a disadvantage.

Richard is not here to say what his disadvantages were. I would say poverty, no solid guidance and a dysfunctional environment. Me, I was at a disadvantage in the same ways as Richard but the main disadvantage for me was growing up in foster care with no love.

Regardless of our disadvantages, Richard and I both were determined to change the game. For Richard that meant doing whatever he had to do to make a change including sacrificing his life.

Richard always looked at selling drugs that way, "Ang, my life is a sacrifice, anything can happen to me. I wanna make sure you can take care of my baby if something happens to me." Those were Richard's words over and over again. I understood what he was saying. I hated when he talked about getting killed or going to jail but it was the truth. When Richard got killed and reality hit, I wasn't prepared but I was prepared. I understood that Richard wanted to make sure the ends justified the means. I never stopped pushing and I can honestly say the ends justified the means and now our family is in a whole different card game.

MOTHER ON HEROIN

❦

The mother that you are born to has everything to do with what you become in life.....Good or Bad but it's your choice believe it or not.

Richard and I grew up in Harlem in the 70's when heroin use was at its climax. Heroin came into the Harlem community and caused a big distraction. By the 80's crack stole what was left. Heroin opened the doors for crack.

Heroin addiction started increasing in the United States in the 1950s. In 1964, The Federal Bureau of Narcotics reported that there was an estimated 48,500 active addicts in the country. Half of all the people addicted to heroin resided in New York City. New York City was called the dope capital and Harlem was the epicenter.

By the 1970s, "junkies" and "feigns" were on every other street corner. There were an estimated 100,000 drug addicts living uptown. I remember walking down Lenox Avenue and seeing the junkies leaned over on their knees. I always wondered how they never fell over. It was quite a scene.

Drug use, unemployment and the high school dropout rate continued to rise. AIDS, hepatitis, and other health problems also rose. The mortality rate, teenage pregnancy, the number of hungry children and crime continued to rise. These were the factors that caused destruction to our community.

The Rockefeller Laws enacted in 1973 were put into place to criminalize the addicts and pushers in the black communities, especially in Harlem. Basically, Rocky called this locking up of addicts as "cleaning up the infestation." That only made things worse. Black men were being sent to prison and leaving their families behind. Addicted mothers were left to maintain and take care of children on their own. More stress was added to many families and it bled out into the streets. All of Harlem was in survival mode. There were two and three families living in a single or two-bedroom apartment. Everyone was living on top of each other but families were still broken up. Grandmothers were trying to keep it together and taking care of all the grandchildren because their own children had become addicted to heroin and were unfit to take care of their children.

Children of addicted parents in Harlem were now the victims, too. All too often, both the mother and the father were addicted. Children were left alone at home to fend for themselves. The oldest child often took on the responsibility of making sure the younger siblings were fed. Mothers were out turning tricks or doing whatever to get their next fix. Fathers were in jail for robbery, burglary and possession of narcotics.

Children were traumatized and being taken from their mothers due to neglect, abuse, and abandonment, and placed into the homes of strangers. In 1974, about 30,000 children were in the foster care system in New York City. That was a disproportionate number of children living away from home compared to the national rate.

Because my momma was a dope fiend, someone reported my mother to the Bureau of Child Welfare also known as BCW. They reported my mother because she left us in the house by ourselves one night so BCW came and took us away.

Let me just give y'all a quick background on my mother. My mother was given away by her mother when she was a baby. The name on her birth certificate says Kathleen Johnson, and they called her Kathy.

It was a time when it was easy to change names on birth certificates and it was easy for my mother to be illegally adopted. I don't really know what my mother's name was. Her biological mother was Caucasian and her father was African American, that's what I was told. Her illegally adopted parents were both middle class African American. I have a picture of my mother, so I know she was very pretty when she was a baby and even prettier as a young lady. I was told when my mother found out she was adopted she was already a teenager and that's when she started acting out, doing drugs and so on. I was told my mother had a lot of brothers and they lived in the projects. I was told a lot of things but I don't know a lot of things for sure.

My mother gave birth to my older sister Leah when she was 16 years old, and she became a dope fiend when she was about 17. I believe she was about 17 because, when I was born, I had to be weaned off of drugs. At that time she was only 18 so I'm guessing she must have started using when she was about 17 years old. By the time she was nineteen, she had three children: me, my sister, and my brother. My youngest brother Leo was born in 1975 six years later. My sister, my brother and I were already in the foster care system when my mother gave birth to my little brother.

My mother's illegally adoptive parents, Nana and Earl, wanted no part of us or my mother when we were taken by BCW. I don't know, maybe they were tired of trying to help my mother stop using heroin. Maybe my mother was an embarrassment to the family. My mother's sister and brother through adoption always seemed to do well for themselves. *Nana and Earl had two children of their own, Aunty Connie and Uncle Billy. Earl was not their biological father but Earl and Nana were married so Earl was their step father. Aunty Connie and Uncle Billy were about 10 years older than my mother and seemed to have very little in common.*

Nana was always very classy. They had just moved into Esplanade Gardens on 147th Street. They lived in building Number Two. Esplanade had just been built and all the upscale black folks were moving there. Back then, if you lived in Esplanade or Lenox Terrace in Harlem, that meant you had a little more than the rest of the folks in Harlem. They would say, "I love your address" if you lived in Esplanade Gardens or Lenox Terrace.

I don't have too many memories of being with my mother before we were put into foster care but I do remember a few moments. Like the time when she was in a drug rehabilitation inpatient center. My siblings and I went to see her and seeing and being with my mother was always fun. I believe we stayed in the Bronx with my Aunt Connie and sometimes with my Uncle Billy when my mom was an inpatient.

One time when we were in the Bronx at my Aunt Connie's house, my sister fell out of the window. I was too young to remember but I've been told the story over and over again. Basically, my sister was going after a ball. The ball went out the window and she went after it. The tree branches and a dumpster saved her life by breaking her fall. I heard that she fell five stories.

Even if I had to see my mom in a drug rehabilitation facility it didn't matter as long as I was with my mother. I can still envision the drug rehabilitation facility. I remember the short brick buildings, green grass, rocky paths from building to building, benches to sit on and a playground for the children who came to see their loved ones.

I remember my mother coming to my school Christmas party when I was in pre-school. My brother Donald and I were both in pre-school at the same time in the same class because we were only 11 months apart. We went to PS 123 right on 140th Street. I still envision my mother walking us down the hill on 141st Street on our way to school.

Whenever my mother would leave us alone at night, I would stay up waiting for her to come back home. When my mother returned, there I was.

I never remember feeling unsafe or angry when my mother left us in the house alone. I missed my mother's love and couldn't wait until she got back home but I never felt unsafe. I do remember being scared of getting my mother in trouble for leaving us alone and being scared that we were going to be taken away.

One night my mother left us alone, as usual. We were living with her on 141st Street on St. Nicholas Avenue. My siblings and I woke up and noticed my mother not there. I'm not sure what happened but I always remember telling them to be quiet before you get mommy in trouble.

My mother always had something sweet to give to me when she got home. Shit she always had something sweet for herself. My mother loved sweets especially candy; I learned later on in life that every heroin addict has a sweet tooth.

As soon as my mother sat down, I would sit on her lap and she would give me candy.

Then she would heat up the heroin, in a pot, using a hot plate on the table, while I sat right in her lap and watched. After the heroin was heated up, my mother tied a rubber cord around her arm so tight and I would watch as she stuck the needle in her arm. I had a front row seat. I never said a word; I just sat there, ate my chocolate and watched.

Sometimes my mother got high by herself but, most of the time, I remember a dark-skinned black man sitting at the table doing the same thing. My mother must have had a thing for dark skinned big men because that's how all of her men looked, with the exception of my father.

I came to understand my mother left us alone, because she was sick not because she didn't love us. She needed to get her fix. Sometimes a person can screw up and coping with the punishment can make things worse but, when it involves children, only the child is really the one who gets hurt. Removing a child from their parents or loved ones because of physical abuse is one thing, but removing them from their parent because of of neglect in my opinion is not always beneficial for the child or the parent. I believe other support services should be put in place to help the parent(s). If you can help a mother, you help a child. Removing a child from what they see as a loving mother or father and placing them into an environment where there is no natural love can affect a child's developmental growth in a number of different areas.

PUT IN THE SYSTEM

O nce a child is put in the foster care system everything becomes systematic and nothing is customized to the child needs, not physically, mentally, or emotionally. Unless the child is blessed to get a foster parent that really knows how to care or tries to care.

After BCW took us from our mother, we were moved to a house in Queens. I remember the lady's name was Mrs. Ruth. I forgot what her husband's name was but they were really mean to us. One time, my siblings and I were sitting at the kitchen table. We had been in this foster home not longer than a week. My brother said, "cheese doodle," and Mrs. Ruth's husband was washing dishes at the sink. He turned around and hit my brother on his head with a plate. The plate broke in half. My brother was only about three years old.

Mrs. Ruth and her husband had older children who would do cruel things to us like wake us up out of our sleep in the middle of the night, "Wake up, wake! Hurry up you late for school, put on your clothes." I used to jump up scared to death and crying at the same time because I could not find my shit. They would also put hot sauce in our mouths while we were asleep or tickle our ears.

I first started being called stupid when I lived with Mrs. Ruth. They always called me stupid because I could not find my shoe or my belt. I hated losing my shit. I also hated being called stupid. I learned to go to God every time I could not find something. I would pray, ask for His help, and whatever I asked for help with, God always answered my request.

We didn't stay in Queens with Mrs. Ruth for long before one of Big Momma's daughters, Mary, became a licensed foster mother and became our foster mother.

Big Momma was a lady from the neighborhood who was known for helping other families out, especially teenage mothers. Big Momma lived in Harlem on 136th Street between Lenox and Adam Clayton Powell Blvd, also known as 7th Avenue. Big Momma had helped my mother take care of us before we were put into foster care. That's what I remember hearing when I was a little girl. I guess if my mother needed a babysitter or if we needed food to eat, she could ask Big Momma. My mother's sister by adoption, Nana's daughter Connie, was friends with one of Big Momma's daughter's, Lori. I'm guessing that's how we got connected to that family.

Big Momma had five daughters of her own and one son: Auntie Colette, Auntie Ray, Aunty Lori, Aunty Lolo, Mary who we called Ma, and Uncle Paul.

Mary was the youngest of Big Mama's daughters and she was the one who signed up to be our foster mother after we were put into the system. Mary always had a very tough look to her. Her look always reminded me of a dyke. That's what we called a woman that looked tough and dressed like a man back then. She always had a mean face and gave off this energy that said, "Don't fuck with me." Mary was quick to slap the shit out of us.

We moved to Jersey City with Mary. Mary lived in a two-family house with her sister, Auntie Colette. We called all Mary's sisters Auntie. Auntie Colette was Big Momma's oldest daughter and Mary's big sister. She was a social worker. Auntie Colette lived in the upstairs apartment alone with her nine children. Betty lived in the downstairs apartment with the five of us. Auntie Colette was a single mother of nine but she always seemed to be organized. Auntie Colette was also a Jehovah's Witness so she was kind of strict. Her children were not permitted to do a lot of things. I never really witnessed any of Auntie Colette's children acting out. They were always so well behaved. I would say at least 8 out of 9 never seemed to give Auntie Colette any problems. We didn't go upstairs to Auntie Colette's house a lot, but once in a blue, one of her daughters would babysit us. Either Holly or Heather would come downstairs to watch us. I loved when either one of them watched us as they both were always so nice to us.

Mary had two children of her own plus my siblings and me; so altogether she had five children to care for.

I lived with Mary for the next eight years of my life.

When we were taken away from my mother, it was traumatic and now my siblings and I were put in a situation that was mentally, verbally, emotionally, and physically abusive. Mary was abusive to her own two children so she definitely didn't care about abusing us. Now that I know what I know, I don't believe she even knew any better. Either way, there was still cause and effect from the abuse that was inflicted upon not only me, but all of us.

So, we were taken from my mother because of neglect and put into foster care only to be abused. It didn't make sense to me. When I think about it now, it was the agency that neglected us, they should have known they were placing my siblings and me in harm's way.

To foster a child is supposed to build them up. We were clearly being broken down. "The Solomon kids," that was us, that was what the foster family called us. Individually, we all had our own names. My sister was called "liar," my brother was called "faggot" and I was called "retarded." I was called retarded so much that I would say it to myself. "You so retarded!" I would say it while hitting myself in the head. I was just six or seven and every time I would forget or lose something I would be so scared. I was scared that Mary was going to scream at me, hit me or call me retarded. I cried every time I could not find something. One day, I was looking for my shoe. I had one shoe on and one shoe off. I could not find the other one. I remember being in the closet crying and talking to myself.

Something told me to stop crying and calm down. I stopped crying and calmed down. Not long after, I found my shoe. I really didn't know what or who—I just know it was a feeling of energy and I heard it say, "Stop crying and calm down." I listened, and it worked.

I spent a lot of time alone with myself when I was a little girl and I loved it. Mary loved sending us to bed as punishment. That was fine with me. I loved going to bed. It was where I dreamed. Every night after dinner we would clean the kitchen, wash the dishes, and dry the silverware, dishes, pots, and pans. Then we would put everything away, wipe the stove off, sweep, and mop the kitchen floor before we cut the light off. Afterwards, we took our baths, put our pajamas on and headed to the living room to watch TV. Mary would sit on the couch, and we would sit on the floor right in front of her. We watched whatever was on. Most of the time it was ABC Nightline that came on right before Jeopardy and then the ABC News.

Our bedtime was 8:30pm so we got to see one prime time show. It's sad, but honestly, I don't remember what shows we used to watch—I was always in another world. Besides, if we turned our head or said a word, Mary would send us to bed. I loved when she sent me to bed and that happened easily for me because the mice running around me would always make me scream. Mary didn't care, she still sent us to bed.

Every night, I dreamed, and every night, my dream continued from the night before.

I had my own story going on with all positive thoughts. I would dream about having my own children and treating them so well. I dreamt about having a husband to love me. I dreamt about going to college and having a house with grass and a pool in the yard, but most of all, I dreamed about living back with my mother. My dreams meant everything to me. My dreams helped me to escape and create a world of my own. I didn't only dream when I went to bed at night—I daydreamed all the time. My teachers would say, "I don't know where she be at because she don't be here." Auntie Colette, Mary's sister, would say I was letting the devil take over my mind, but I knew that was a lie. My days were filled with screams and dreams as I always found myself drifting off into another world.

After we were "settled" with Mary, the Bureau of Child Welfare made arrangements for our mother to see us. At first, we had to go downtown to this big building. I remember getting off the elevator and a kind social worker meeting us. Mary was a changed person in front of the social worker as she escorted my siblings and me to a room that was full of books and toys. There were tables and chairs, so we sat right down scared to touch a thing. My mother walked in the room.

I was just six years old, but I can still see the smile on her face.

I'm not sure what my expression was because most of the time I was expressionless, but inside, my heart was filled with joy. I was so happy to see my mother. She hugged us, gave us kisses, and told us how much she loved us. When it was time to leave, I always wanted to cry but I had to keep it inside or else Mary would curse me out.

"Shut the fuck up. She don't care about you. She ain't nothing but a drug addict," were the words we heard all the time. As soon as we got back to Mary's home, I would go back into my shell and talk to myself and my God within.

A lot was happening during those years. We moved to four different apartments with Mary. We moved from Jersey City to Harlem, then we moved from Harlem to upstate New York to a small town named Valley Cottage, and after that, we moved back to Harlem.

After a while my mother was able to get visitation rights and eventually she was able to take us on the weekend. The first time my mother was able to take us for the weekend was when we lived in Harlem on 159th St and St. Nicholas Avenue. We moved there from Jersey City after my foster mother Mary stabbed her husband in the eye. I can't remember the whole story, but I remember she stabbed him in the eye and after that we moved to Harlem. Aunty Lori, Mary's sister, helped her get the apartment.

Auntie Lori always had connections and was always able to get the hook up on just about anything. Auntie Lori was connected to some

Italian guy and she owned her own number spot in Harlem on 136th St between 7th and 8th Avenue. She was known in Harlem as "The Queen of Harlem." Auntie Lori was smart, owned a business, had a pretty face, nice shape, small waist and she dressed her ass off. Auntie Lori didn't play no games and was about getting the bag.

The first weekend my mother was able to take us was the first time I met my little brother. I was about 7 years old, and he was like one going on two years old.

My mother would come and get us from Harlem and take us to Queens with her on the weekends. She lived in Jamaica, Queens in an apartment building right under some railroad tracks.

As soon as I stepped foot out of my foster mother's home and was with my mother, I felt like I was in heaven. We would all walk from 159th on St. Nicholas Avenue to 155th Street and St. Nicholas to the C train to Jamaica Queens. There were my siblings, me, my mother and her friend. I remember my mother always having a male friend with her. I can't remember if it was always the same male friend, but I do remember my mother always being with a male. Before we got on the train, we always stopped at the pizza parlor on 155th Street and St. Nicholas to get pizza. They had the best pizza and the slices were really big.

After we finished eating our pizza, we got right on the C train and headed to Queens where my mother lived. It was the best train ride to me. I always had so much fun. My mother always let my siblings and me swing around on the train poles. She let us do whatever we wanted to do. Now that I'm a mom I know it was her guilt, the guilt of not being with us that stopped her from disciplining us.

When we got to Queens my mother would take us to her friends' house so they could see us. She would show us off and be so happy. "Look at my kids," she would say.

My mother never mistreated us or called us mean names. I always felt comfortable and loved when I was with my mother. I remember one day we were on the train going to Queens. It was my mother, her male friend, my siblings and me. My siblings were running around on the train. Yes, people were looking at them like they were crazy but my mother didn't give a fuck. Me, I was sitting down. I was always very quiet and to myself. I sat on the train with my mother and her male friend. I sat right next to her like a little puppy. I'll never forget the day I heard my mom tell her friend, "This is my B-E-S-T," as she held me tight. It was during one of our train rides to Queens on the C train. I remember it clearly. I didn't know what "B-E-S-T" spelled so I asked someone, and they told me. I forget who I asked but I remember asking and being told it spelled, "Best." I was around 7 years old. Yea, I probably should have known but spelling and reading have never been my favorite subjects. I'm a math girl all day long.

I hated when it was time to leave my mother and go back to Mary's house. I guess it kind of felt like being bipolar. One minute my energy was up and the next minute my energy was at zero.

Being with my mother felt natural, loving, comfortable and it was always happiness to be with her. Going back to Mary's house brought my spirit down and made me anxious. I used to be filled with fear. The only time I really felt safe is when I went to sleep at night. I felt safe in my dreams. It was the only place I could express myself.

I was happy that my youngest brother was able to stay with my mother. I used to wish it was me. But it wasn't long before BCW found a reason to take him too. I'm not sure what happened but I do remember the day my foster mother Mary and her sister Lolo drove out to Queens. They didn't even know where my mother lived but they made it their business to find out. They claimed they wanted to make sure my little brother was ok. My little brother was about 2 or 3 years old at this time. Not too long after that day my youngest brother was living with us also. I'm not sure what exactly happened because every time we were with my mother she took care of him well, in my eyes anyway. My mother took care of all of us when we were with her. She always gave us love.

Mary and Lolo were good friends with the social workers. The social workers never seemed to have our best interest, instead they seemed to have the best interest of the foster parent. I hated that they took my brother. I hated that he was going to be called names like I was. Only difference was that my brother did not mind getting himself into trouble. He do dumb shit like fuck up in school. Whenever he had a test in school,he would put the craziest answers down. He did it on purpose so Aunty Lolo thought he was crazy. But that didn't stop Aunty Lolo from hitting upside his head all the time. Whatever she had in her hand was what my brother got hit ith, a pot, a big spoon, a spoon, a hanger, a plate, whatever. It always seemed like my brother was getting hit. He was diagnosed with ADHD so they were able to get extra money for him. They were not trained nor skilled at provide the type of car he needed. His mental health is still not right today.

I don't remember much about my father. His parental rights were terminated when I was a little girl. I really don't remember how old I was when his rights were terminated but I remember it happening. I remember going downtown to family court or maybe it was to the Bureau of Child Welfare. I was aware of what was going on and I knew his rights were being terminated. My father was also addicted to heroin and I never remember him being around when I was a little girl, so I'm sure his rights were being terminated for neglect. I remember being asked some questions by a few people. I'm guessing they were the social workers and the lawyers. I don't remember what questions they asked but I do remember being in favor of my father's rights being terminated. I was happy his rights were being terminated because I was afraid of my father, I didn't like him.

I remember going to see my father one time and after that I never wanted to see him again. We kids went to visit him at his mother's house in the Bronx . The social worker dropped us off for a visit. It was an overnight visit. The only time I could ever remember spending the night with my father or his mother.

I remember lying in the bed next to my father and feeling uncomfortable. I remember he touched me in a way that made me feel uncomfortable. I can't remember how he touched me or where he touched me. I just remember he touched me and it felt uncomfortable. It's weird, it's like having an itch but you don't know where to scratch. I'm sure that situation is the very reason I have always been very timid in general whenever I had to deal with older men. I remember one time this man that we called our uncle asked me for a hug and I broke out crying.

The next time I saw my father was when I was a little older. I think I was about 12 years old. My brother and I were walking down 140th Street between 7th and 8th Avenue. My brother noticed my father. He was in front of a number spot across the street. My brother said, "C'mon, I'm going across the street to ask him for a dollar." I said, "I don't want to go." My brother went across the street. I knelt down and hid behind the car. I didn't want to see my father and I did not want him to see me.

My father looked like he was high off of heroin but that did not stop my brother. I can't remember if he had a dollar to give my brother or not and I did not care. My father's rights were terminated and I never really cared because my father never gave me good vibes.

We lived on 159th street and St. Nicholas Avenue for about three years and then Mary moved upstate to Rockland County to a town called Valley Cottage. My mother did not come to see us as much once we moved upstate. I guess it was hard for her to get there. I don't know, I'm just making an assumption. If I was making decisions at the foster care agencies, I would not allow foster parents to move so far away from the child's biological parents.

When we lived upstate Mary had to work every Saturday, so her niece Donna would come over to watch us. It used to be crazy. Sometimes it was fun and irresponsible, and then there were times when Donna used to smoke weed and drink and she let my siblings and me smoke weed right along with her. I was about 9 years old smoking a joint. I would take three pulls and be laughing for the rest of the day.

My siblings were always good at shoplifting. We lived right off Route 303 next to The Food Emporium grocery store. Donna would let my sister and brother go to the store to shoplift. They would come back with wine coolers and all types of goodies. We had a party almost every Saturday.

When it was time for Mary to come home that's when shit started to get serious. It was time to clean up and that's when Donna had to get things in control, so she got quite bossy. I remember one time she hit my head with the telephone handle. I can't remember exactly what happened, but I do remember trying to call for help.

We lived in Valley Cottage for 4 years before Mary moved us back to Harlem. This time we moved to 629 Lenox Avenue. Between 141st Street and 142nd Street on Lenox Avenue. I was 12 years old, in the 7th grade and I went to I.S. 136 which was right on 136th Street on Edgecomb Avenue.

I WAS A GOOD GIRL

I thought if I never lied, we would move back with my mother, I never thought my mother was going to die. I used to wonder, Is this how God rewards me for being a good girl, by taking my mother away?

Once we moved back to Harlem my mother came to get us almost every weekend. She stopped using heroin and was in the process of getting us back. We were going to live back with my mom soon. That's what I thought and that's what I wanted to think. True or false I was believing that we were going to move back with my mother. I was so happy inside. Then my mother died.

My siblings and I were with my mother the weekend before she died. It was a weekend I will never forget. My mother wanted to take us to the movies or roller skating. I can't remember which one. She promised to take us but when the time came for us to go, she could not take us because she didn't have any money. We were sitting in a pizza parlor right under a train station in Jamaica Queens. It was my sister and my two brothers and me. My sister got upset with my mother and my mother started to cry. "I love y'all, I love y'all," my mother cried the words, "I love y'all," over and over again. I wanted to jump up, hug her, and say I love you too, but I didn't. When I was a little girl, I did not talk much. I was a late talker and I had to go to speech class 3 times a week, so I never liked to talk. I had a hard time pronouncing words and my siblings used to make fun of me all the time so most of the time I would sit there and not say shit.

My mother died, and I never got the chance to tell her I loved her. Never again will I hold back from telling my loved ones I love them.

I still remember the day Mary called us into her bedroom. I don't know how my siblings felt but I was always scared whenever Mary called us into her bedroom. My siblings and I walked in the room and stood in a line right next to each other facing Mary. "Yes Ma," we all said at the same time. We sounded so bland and hollow which was how we felt inside. Mary looked at us and said, "Your mother died."

I ran in the bathroom, slammed the door and I locked the door. I sat on the toilet crying. I talked to God.

I was fresh with boys when I was younger. I used to hump the bed and look for men and women kissing on TV but other than that I was good. I never lied, I always told the truth. Mary came to the door, "Open the door Angela." I cried and I cried. I didn't lie, I cried out loud. But I didn't lie, I said it over and over again. I couldn't understand why God took my mother when I was being a good girl.

I don't remember much about my mother's funeral. I remember seeing her in a beautiful casket that looked like a little girl's bedding. Her hair was in a half up half down style with Shirley Temple curls. The Funeral was at Mother Zion Church on 137th Street between Lenox and

Seventh Avenue. The day of the funeral I ran out of church. That's all I can remember. I think Aunty Lori ran after me but, honestly, I don't know. I just remember someone came behind me.   I don't remember how my siblings reacted to my mother's death but I'm sure they were devastated just like me. We never really found out how my mother died. I remember overhearing my foster mother say that she got sick at a cook out in Queens and when she went to the hospital they gave her the wrong medication. No one ever followed up so it was never confirmed how my mother really died.

At the time, no one asked us if we were alright. No one cared about how we felt, not even the social workers. There was no therapy involved at all. Everything just went back to normal. The name calling and all the other ugly stuff that came along with living in Mary's household. Mary never told us she loved us. As a matter of fact, the only person I can remember ever saying I love you to me when I was a little girl was my mother and now she was gone.

After my mother died, I decided that would never stay in any home that I did not like.   I ran away from Mary's home not long after my mother died. After that I ran away from every home that BCW placed me in if I felt badly treated in any way.

I started cutting school, I got a penis penetrated into my vagina for the first time and I eventually ran away from Mary's home.

There were no days to grieve and no time to heal when my mother died. My siblings and I went back to school almost immediately.   There was no compassion in the home and there was no compassion at school. Soon after my mother died, a boy in my class said to me,"That's why your mother died." His name was Chuck. Chuck was bad and he did not care what came out of his mouth. I forgot why he said what he said but it was mean. He said it in front of the whole class and I cried. I was twelve years old in the seventh grade, my mother had just died and I was living in foster care. That's enough for any child to have a breakdown. I didn't want to go to school after being embarrassed and crying in front of the whole class. I started cutting school with my brother. My brother Donald always looked out for me when we were younger, even though he was eleven months younger. Donald and I went to the same school so it was easy for us to cut together. Donald was always very smart in school, much smarter than I was. Learning came naturally for him; I had to have a tutor to help me with my school work.

Donald and I would get on the train and go to 42nd Street. He loved playing the arcade games. Just about every store on 42nd was a game room or a porn shop back in the 80's. We always looked for a game room that was crowded with a lot of people. We needed to be out of sight so the truant officers would not see us.

We always had money because my brother would steal Mary's money while she was asleep at night. Mary kept her pocketbook on the floor between her nightstand and her bed. Right where she laid her head. My brother would get on his knees and crawl around Mary's bed to her pocketbook. She kept a lot of money in her pocketbook because she worked in a number spot. Now that I think about it, it was probably the bank. My brother would steal at least $50 dollars all the time. Sometimes it would be a hundred dollar bill and sometimes it would be a fifty dollar bill, either way it was a red flag. What little child walked around with a fifty or hundred dollar bill in their pocket in the 80's? So Donald and I always waited until we were downtown before we spent the money.

Most of the time when I cut school, I went downtown with my brother but other times I would just wait around and go back home. Donna, Mary's niece, was staying with us so she was always there to open the door. Donna didn't care if we cut school.   Donna was giving her mother Colette a hard time so they thought it would be a good idea for Donna to stay with us in Harlem. Donna also stayed with us when we lived upstate in Valley Cottage. Donna was older than all of us so whenever Mary needed a sitter for us, Donna was already there. . .

I lost my virginity hanging out with Donna. I went to Jersey City with her one time   to see her boyfriend. She told me he had a friend for me, and I couldn't wait to go. Being fresh sexually was like the only thing I did wrong when I was a little girl. It was also a way for me to fit in.   Donna and I talked about me having sex with this guy before we even planned to go, and I agreed.

So one day instead of going downtown with my brother to the game room I met Donna at the path train on 34th street and we went to Jersey City. When we got to Donna's boyfriend house, he was there with another guy, the guy I agreed to fuck. He was chocolate with a nice body and a cute face but he was much older than me. I was 12 years old, he had to be older than eighteen. We all sat on the couch for a little while. They smoked some weed and shortly after Donna and her boyfriend went into one of the bedrooms. We stayed sitting on the couch. Then he got up off the couch and said "Come on," and, as he was getting up, he took my hand. I didn't say anything I just followed. He led me into a different bedroom that was empty with just a bed and a little radio. I sat down on the bed as soon as we went in the room. He put on the radio but nothing was playing but commercials, so he popped in a music cassette.   The music came on and he sat down next to me on the bed.

He pushed me back gently on the bed and began to kiss me. One of his hands went up my shirt and underneath my training bra, he began to play with my nipples and my vagina began to quench.

He grabbed my vagina with his other hand, and I started to squirm. It was feeling good until he started to unbutton my pants; that's when I began to get scared. That's when I realized I was not ready. I was used to touching, humping, and having an orgasm from just the feeling but I had never had a penis inside of my vagina before.

I was scared but how could I tell him to stop?   I was the one who wanted to come and agreed to have sex.   I knew the plan and I didn't want to disappoint anyone, the guy, Donna or Donna's boyfriend so I continued to go along. After my pants were unbuttoned, he stood up and took his pants off.   I could tell his penis was hard because it was kind of large. He pulled my pants down from the top and underneath my butt, them he pulled them all the way off. He took my panties off the same way and threw them on the floor. He pulled his boxers down as he crawled up between my legs and opened them wide. He rubbed his penis on my vagina for a few seconds before he tried to push it in, his penis would not go in so he pushed hard. My vagina was closed tight and it was hard for his penis to get in. I hadn't even got my menstruation yet and my vagina was being penetrated by a man I didn't even know. I could feel his penis ripping my vagina open. I said "It hurts" over and over again but I guess I didn't say it loud or aggressive enough because he didn't stop.   He just kept pushing until his penis finally busted my vagina open. Then up and down sticking his penis in and out of me while I lay there thinking, Is this what sex is supposed to feel like?

By the time we all got finished fucking, it was time to go. Donna and I took the path train back to the city, we got home on time and that was it. I don't actually remember ever knowing his name and I never saw him again after that day.

My brother and I cut school for more than two weeks straight before Mary found out that we were not going to school. One day Mary went to our school. I forget why she went to the school but I know that's how she found out about us not going to school.

As soon as my brother and I got home, Donna said, "Mary knows that y'all didn't go to school, y'all in trouble and y'all betta not say y'all stayed here." My brother and I were like oh shit. We promised Donna that we wouldn't say anything about coming back home instead of going to school. We promised that we would tell Mary that we went downtown to 42nd Street everyday to the game room. I also promised to never say anything about going to Jersey City to see her boyfriend and getting fucked.

I was sure, that as soon as Mary walked through the door, she was going to start beating me and my brother's ass. But that's not what happened. Mary called us into the living room. My brother and I both walked into the living room at the same time. Mary was sitting on the couch smoking a cigarette. She smoked Kools and everyday she got home that was the first thing she did, sit on the couch and have a cigarette. She loved smoking. I remember Mary whopping our asses with a cigarette in her hand. My brother and I stood in front of her looking stupid.

"Why haven't you two been going to school?" I shrugged my shoulders to say I don't know, my brother did the same. "Where have you two been going?" I answered "Downtown to 42nd Street." "How did you get to 42nd street with no money," Mary asked. "We hopped the train," my brother said, and I nodded my head to agree with what my brother said. "Neither of you better miss another day of school. Skip school again, and I'm going to whop the shit out of you, go to bed!" I immediately left the living room and my brother followed. I was so happy that we did not get our ass whipped. As soon as I got in the room I lay down, went to sleep, and from that day on I never missed a day of junior high school.

ON MY OWN

Once I got to high school I was ready to leave Mary's home. I was thirteen years old.

When my mother died something inside of me said you are in control of your own destiny. I only had my God within and it was He that I depended on most of the time, so I trusted what I felt inside most of the time.

I ran away to Nana and Earl's house, my mother's adoptive parents, in Esplanade Gardens, on 147th Street in Harlem, a few blocks away from where I lived with Mary. I planned the runaway. I waited until Friday after school before I made a move. I wanted to make sure I didn't have school the next day. I figured I would have the whole weekend to persuade Nana and Earl to let me live with them.

They weren't my mother's biological mother and father but they were the only grandparents I knew. When the Bureau of Child Welfare took us from my mother for neglect, Nana and Earl did not take us in. I'm not sure why and I'm not going to lie. Now I can see how a mother would want nothing to do with a drug addict child or their kids. It's emotional and a traumatic situation for all involved.

I wasn't sure how Nana was going to respond to me running away to her home. Especially after constantly hearing how she and Earl didn't want us. Every opportunity Mary got she would remind us that our family didn't want us. "They don't want y'all if they wanted y'all then you all would be living with them." I didn't care what Mary said; all the memories I had of Nana and Earl were loving. True, Nana and Earl did not take us to live with them, but Nana and Earl came to get us on the holidays. We spent Christmas with them and on Easter Sunday they made sure we were all dressed up. When the Jackson Five came to Madison Square Garden my siblings and I were there because Nana and Earl took us to see them. We went Ice Skating at Rockefeller Center. How many children of color living in the hood back then can say they went skating at Rockefeller Center? Not too many. Whenever I was with Nana and Earl, I always felt comfortable, relaxed, at peace and loved. That was the life I wanted so I took my chances and ran away to Nana's home.

It was my first time running away and I was a little nervous, but I was determined to leave. I ran down the stairs and out of the building. It was the beginning of December 1983 right before Christmas. It was cold and dark outside. I walked straight up Lenox Avenue until I reached Esplanade Gardens on 147th Street. Esplanade Garden has six buildings, three of them are right off Lenox Avenue and the other three are between Lenox and Seventh Avenue between 147th Street and 149th Street. 2569 7th Avenue was her address, apartment 18L. I didn't remember what apartment she lived in, but I knew her name. When I got to Nana's building I looked on the name directory. The doorman watched me through the glass as I rang Nana's bell. Nana answered, "Who is it?" she asked in a polite tone. "Angela," I said, sounding like I was questioning myself. Nana said, "Who?" "Angela," I said, only this time I said it a little louder the same way. The door buzzed, thank God I thought. I pushed the door open. I signed the log in book for the building and the door man told me which way to go. Nana lived on the 18th floor, so that meant I needed to get on one of the elevators that stopped on the even floors. Esplanade buildings were beautiful and well taken care of. All of the apartments that I had lived in were all walk ups, dirty, smelly and you had to watch out for boogers when you held on to the stair rail. Esplanade was luxury compared to the buildings I was used to living in. Esplanade had doormen, pretty tiles and mirrors in the lobby. It was so clean and the building smelled like nothing but expensive fragrance; even inside of the elevator it smelled so good.   As soon as I got off the elevator, I saw Nana standing at her apartment door.

Nana had on a beautiful satin house gown, her hair was jet black and I could not help but notice how pretty she was. I adored the lady Nana was because she had so much class, always lady like and polite. Nana didn't allow me to get on or off the elevator without saying Hello, Good morning, Have a nice day or Good night. That's just how Nana was; anything else in her eyes was rude and not polite.

Nana gave me a kiss and a hug and told me to come in. As soon as I stepped foot in the door it felt like heaven, another one of my special moments. Nana was alone because Earl was at work. Nana's energy was welcoming. She took my coat and told me to have a seat on the couch in the living room. I sat on the couch as Nana hung my coat in the closet. As I sat on the couch, I admired how beautiful Nana's apartment was. The carpet was blue and the walls were covered with white wallpaper designed with blue velour that felt like suede. Next to the patio was a bar with all types of spirits and on every table there was a pretty bowl filled with nuts and a nut cracker.

Nana came and sat on the couch next to me.   "What are you doing here?" Nana asked. "I don't wanna live with Mary anymore." I started to cry, "She does not treat me nice. I'm sick of being called retarded and out of my name. I don't wanna stay there anymore can I please stay here with you and Earl?" I asked.

Nana said, "Well I have to see what Earl says, let's wait until he gets home from work."

Earl got home around eleven o'clock. He worked at a grocery store downtown. Earl was the security guard, and he worked the night shift. When he got home Nana and I were still awake. Earl already kind of knew what was going on because Nana had spoken to him during his lunch break.

Nana and I were sitting at the dining table talking. Nana was telling me how she got my mother. "Your mother was a beautiful little baby. I was working on 132nd Street for a pediatrician. His name was Dr. Liggins. I was the receptionist and one day this white lady was leaving the office with a newborn baby. It was your mother." I said, "Oh my God that's a beautiful baby let me have her." Nana said the lady said, "Ok I will be back." Nana said the white lady came back, spoke to Dr. Liggins and put my mother in her arms. "After the white lady gave your mother to me Dr. Liggins changed your mother's birth certificate to Kathleen Johnson. He also told me your mother's father was a dark-skinned black man." Nana never told me what my mother's real name was and I never asked. I didn't want to seem like I was being greedy for information, honestly I was happy that she was telling me that much.

I was already dressed for bed because Nana had already given me something to sleep in. "Take a shower and put these night clothes on," she said. After I got out of the shower, Nana showed me the room I would be sleeping in. There was a twin-size bed, a desk, and a set of drums. In the closet were nothing but men's suits. It was not hard to tell this was the room Earl used to do his own thing. When Nana and I were talking she told me all about she and Earl's younger life. Nana said she danced at the Savoy and Earl played the drums in the service and he also played with Count Basie. So that explained the drum set and all the other music equipment that was in the room. It was not hard to tell that my grandfather loved music.

Earl hung his coat up, washed his hands and came to the dining room with bags filled with groceries. Earl always brought groceries home, there was never one night he came home empty handed.

Earl stood in the kitchen putting the groceries away. "What's going on Angela? Bundles told me you wanna stay here." Bundles is what Earl called Nana. Nana said he called her Bundles because when they first me he always said she was a bundle of joy. "I wanna stay here because Mary does not treat us nice. She has never treated us nice," I said. "Does Mary know where you are at?" "No, we didn't call her yet," Nana said. "Ok well the right thing to do is to call Mary and let her know where you're at. " Earl picked up the phone and called Mary. "Hi Mary, how are you? I'm calling to let you know Angela is over here. Bundles and I are talking to her. We will give you a call in the morning." That night Nana, Earl and I stayed up until about one in the morning talking about how life was for me at Mary's house. They both said they had no idea that my sisters and I were being mistreated. Before we went to sleep Earl and Nana decided to let me live with them.

The next morning, I opened my eyes, and lay there for a moment. I was in disbelief, it was like I said to myself oh shit I'm still here. I remember that morning, the sun was shining bright, even through the window blinds you could tell the sky was clear. Nana knocked on the door, "Yes?" I answered. She cracked the door open. "I left you a new toothbrush and a face cloth on the bathroom sink. Brush your teeth, wash your face and come eat breakfast."

About a minute after Nana closed the door, I got up. I put on the bathrobe and slippers she gave me the night before. Then I went to the bathroom to brush my teeth and wash my face. Afterwards I headed to the dining room for breakfast. When I got there, Earl was already sitting down at the table. "Good morning," I said. "Well look who's up," Earl said joking. "I already spoke to Mary. I told her we agreed to let you live with us. She seemed really upset that we said yes, but anyway I told her we would get in touch with BCW first thing Monday morning." I was so relieved and happy that my grandfather took care of everything without me having to be present. Talking to Mary always made me nervous. Nana was in the kitchen frying some breakfast sausage. "I'm making pancakes and sausages but we have hot and cold cereal it you want." "What kind of cereal?" "We have frosted flakes and rice crispy." "Oh I'll have Frosted Flakes please.""Ok, you want me to heat up the milk?" " Heat up the milk?" I asked. I had never seen anybody heat up milk and put it on cold cereal. "Yes it taste good when you heat up the milk, try it and see if you like it". " Ok I'll try." Nana passed me a bowl. "Get the cereal out of this cabinet and get a spoon out of the drawer right there." Nana pointed to the drawer with the silverware. "Let me heat up the milk." I poured my Frosted Flakes in the bowl and sat down at the table. When Nana was done heating up the milk, she poured it over my cereal. I took one spoonful and it was really good. Nana and Earl did a few cool things in the kitchen that I had never experienced. Like Nana used to love to make ice cream soda pops. Nana had the tall glasses some of them curvy and some of them not. She had the colorful straws that were twisted like a knot. She made ice cream soda pops with vanilla ice and coke cola. I loved to watch the ice cream fuzz up and float over. Earl kept 7up soda and cherry syrup so we could make Shirley Temple drinks and he never made one drink without a cherry on top. Oh how I was in heaven living with my Nana and Earl.

The weekend was over and Monday morning came. Earl called BCW, the Bureau of Child Welfare, to let the social worker know I was there. When Earl called, the social worker was already aware. I'm guessing Mary had to call and let them know where I was as soon as she found out. Earl told the social worker that I said I wanted to live with them. He confirmed that it was ok. So the social worker said it should not be a problem since they were my grand mother and grand father. A few days later the social worker called and said they were told that they were not my real grand parents. The social worker said since they were never legally my mother's adoptive parents they would have to become licensed foster parents. Nana and Earl said no problem and the process of them becoming my foster parents started.

It was right before Christmas when I started living with Nana and Earl. Nana asked me what I wanted for Christmas. I told her I would like to have a sheep skin coat. Nana asked my grandfather Earl if I could get a sheep skin and Earl said it was ok as long as it didn't cost more than two hundred bucks. I was so excited because I liked sheep skin coats and it was the type of coat everyone was wearing. Shearlings is still my favorite type of fur coat. So one Sunday after church right before Christmas, Nana and Earl surprised me. I didn't know where Earl was driving to and I didn't ask any questions. Nana and Earl always went out on the weekends shopping. Earl took Nana where ever she wanted to go and I followed along. Especially on Sundays because I had no choice because we would go right after church. I remember when Earl pulled up in front of the sheep skin store. The store was right off of Delancey on one of the side streets. I forget the name of the store but I know it was popular back then. Nana and I got out of the car and went inside. Earl sat in the car looking over his number slips. Most of the sheep skins were two hundred dollars back then. Most people had tan, brown, or black, so as soon as I saw them, I said, "Nana I want that one." "Which one?" "The gray one right there." I pointed to the grey sheep skin hanging up on the top row. It was a three quarter sheep skin for two hundred dollars. I was happy because Earl had already told me two hundred dollars was my spending limit. The sales guy got the grey sheep skin down from the top rack, "Size small right? Yeah a small, here you go," he passed me the coat. I tried the coat on. "I like it, it looks nice," Nana said. I looked in the mirror and liked the way the coat looked on me. I was so happy I was able to get what I wanted. Nana went inside her change purse and handed me $200 to take to the cashier.

Spending that Christmas with Nana and Earl was very special and not because of the sheep skin coat. It was the first time I was able to relax and enjoy the Christmas holiday like a child. I received toys and clothes on Christmas Day with Mary. But I was never able to enjoy the toys or clothes on Christmas Day because I was never comfortable, I was always scared that Mary was going to scream and call me names.

The new year came in and everything was going great. Nana and Earl told me I had to join their church choir so I did. Every Saturday I had to go to choir practice or stay in the house all day. Of course, I went to practice every Saturday and then from there I was able to stay outside with my friends. I met a few friends from Esplanade, gals and guys and we would go downtown to Macy's just about every weekend. We rode the escalators up and down in Macy's all day.

We stayed mostly in the electronic section listening to music on the radios, and we competed against each other to see who could type the fastest on the typewriters. After Macy's we went to McDonald's to have lunch. In 1980 you could get a whole meal from McDonald's for less than three dollars, a burger, fries, and a milk shake instead of a soda.

Living with Nana and Earl was really becoming my world. Everything was not always peaches and cream but it was my dream. I never dreamed of life being perfect but I did dream of having proper love and care. Just to be talked to nice and a chance to express myself comfortably is what I always dreamed of, and Nana and Earl gave that to me. Even when I cut class or came in the house after my curfew, Nana or Earl never cursed me or called me out of my name. Nana told me I could not go outside for a week and to stop with the crocodile tears if I cried but she never made me feel like shit.

About eight months after I started staying with Earl and Nana, I noticed Nana started forgetting, almost everything. Nana forgot where she put her money, her keys, and she forgot who my social worker was when she came for a visit.

"I can't find my purse." "What purse, Nana?" "My little purse that I have all the time." "Nana where's the last place you had it?" I would ask. Just about every night and day this is what Nana and I went through.

Nana had a little table in the foyer area, and she had a bowl that sat on top of the table. Whenever her friends visited her from the building, they would drop their keys in the bowl as soon as they came through the door. One night Nana moved her friend's keys and put them some place and could not remember where she'd put them. It took us three hours before we found Nana friend's keys and her friend was able to go home to her own apartment.

I felt so bad for Nana because she would cry whenever she could not find something. She didn't want my grandfather Earl to know that something was going on with her memory; she never told him and neither did I.

Nana's memory got worse as the months passed by. The foster care procedure was still going on and Nana and Earl had not yet officially become my foster grandparents.

A few months after the summer of 1984, I had to move from Nana and Earl's house because Nana was diagnosed with amnesia. The summer was over and school was back in session. I was in the 10th grade and just 15 years old. One day when I was in school the social worker came to the house for a visit and Nana did not know who she was. The Bureau of Child Welfare found their home unfit and told me I had to be moved to another foster home. I was so hurt. It was the first time I'd felt free. I cried and cried and begged the social worker to stay with my grandmother. I told them I could take care of Nana but the social worker said that was not my responsibility.

The social worker said that I could stay with Mary's sister Lolo. Aunty Lolo lived upstate New York in Rockland County in a little town called Nanuet. Lolo always wanted a girl. She had two foster children of her own, a boy and a girl, but the girl acted more like a boy. I was girly girly and I knew Aunty Lolo liked that I was girly girly so I thought there was a chance that she would treat me nice. I was wrong. Aunty Lolo's home wasn't that much different than Mary's, she also called me out of my name and I didn't like it.

One day she called me a retarded bitch and I said, "I'm not a retarded bitch." I told her she was a retarded bitch and walked out the front door.

It was spring 1985, the weather was starting to get nice. I didn't have to worry about staying warm so I didn't take a whole lot of clothes. I left for good.

I walked fast through the woods to the Nanuet mall bus stop. The Nanuet mall bus stop was one of the main bus stops in Rockland County. There were buses going into the city all the time and. I got on the bus to 42nd Port Authority. I was scared and worried that someone would look at me, notice that I was a little girl, mind my business, and call the police. I was 15 years old but I looked like I was about 12 years old. I always looked younger than my age. I didn't want anyone to call the police so I would put my hoodie on and go to the back seat of the bus. I was a red flag in my mind but somehow I always made it to the city without anyone stopping me.

I stayed with different friends when I got to the city. I never had a problem finding some place to stay and, if I didn't, I would just ride the train back and forth until I figured something out.

The summer came, I was still on the run, bouncing from one friend's home to the next. Harlem was popping and I was trying not to have to go to some foster home. It was the year of 1985 and there was a block party every Saturday. Well, actually the block that I was from seemed to have a block party every day and night. The streets would be filled with kids. The sidewalks would be lined up with chairs as the parents sat and watched. We would stay out late, jumping rope, playing tops, jacks or hop scotch and listening to music.

Nanuet was boring compared to Harlem. After staying with Nana and Earl, I got used to going to the school yard jams with Dougie Fresh doing the human beat box and Master Don spitting lyrics. I wanted to be outside. I got addicted to the fun.

I was on the run for the spring and summer of 1985 and I stayed out of sight so the people in Harlem who knew my foster family did not see me. I did not want anyone to call BCW and did not want to hear that my foster family was looking for me or my social worker. Whenever I ran away, they would put out an amber alert, well it felt like an amber alert.

The guys from 142nd Street used to say, "Damn Ang, we seen your face on the milk carton," whenever I would show up. In the 1980's faces of missing children were put on the milk cartons. It was the missing children milk carton campaign.

Most of the time when I ran away, I stayed with one of my girlfriends and then there were times when I stayed with random guys until I was in this guy's apartment and someone tried to rob it. I was scared to death.

Dude locked me in the apartment so he could go hustle on the corner. His name was Shaffer and he was from 149th Street. He had one of those locks that required a key to unlock the door to get out. He locked me in. I'm sure he didn't lock me in on purpose. I just think he felt, "She is a runaway she ain't going nowhere." I wasn't going anywhere but when I saw a motherfucker standing on his fire escape, I was scared and wanted to get out. I tried to get out of the apartment, but I did not have a key. It was so crazy because there was a Pit Bull in the room right next to the room that I was in and the Pit Bull never barked. I heard some noise by the window so I peeked out the window and I saw someone standing on the window sill in between the two windows with his back against the wall. I acted like I didn't see the person. I looked around for weapons but there were none. There was a bunch of cleaning products and a mop bucket. I combined all types of cleaning products in the mop bucket. I put on a pot of water to boil. If he came through that window, I was going to be ready for him. I kept going to the door hoping that Shaffer would come back. I started to cry. I wrote on a piece of paper, "Somebody help me" and slipped it under the door to the hallway. I was so scared. Finally, I heard keys. Part of me was scared and part of me was happy. What if it's someone got the guy's keys? The locks turned and the door opened. It was him. It was the guy I was staying with. I held him so tight and told him what I witnessed. He went in the room and there were chips of paint all over the floor. The window was painted down and the person was trying to scrape the paint away so they could open up the window. I stayed the night with him but the next day I got up and left. That was the last time I stayed with a random guy.

September came fast that year. It was time to go back to school and I had to do something because not going to school was not an option. And going back to Nanuet was definitely not an option either. In order for me to go to another school I would need to be registered by a legal guardian.

So I asked Helen if I could stay with her. Helen was Mary's cousin. Helen had two daughters, Yvette and Netta. Helen, Yvette, and Netta lived right around the corner when I lived with Mary at 629 Lenox Avenue. The building we lived in was between 141st and 142nd Street on Lenox Avenue. And Helen lived on 142nd Street in building 100 between Seventh and Lenox Avenue. Once in a while, Mary would let me go around the corner and visit Helen, Yvette, and Netta—but not too much—because she always said Helen was too loose with Yvette and Netta. Mary said Helen let Yvette and Netta do what they wanted to do. In my opinion, Mary was too strict and mean for no reason. I loved going over to Helen's. It was always a busy house. Helen always made sure Yvette and Netta had up-to-date technology. Atari, video music box, a stereo system, a telephone, and kept a kitchen filled with goodies. Every time I went around Helen's house, she would tell me to go get a treat out of the kitchen. I would lie in the bed with Helen and watch TV. I was always comfortable with Helen.

Helen always treated us well. Not only was she nice to me, she was nice to my brother.

Helen always made sure we had lunch money   Mary never gave us lunch money and Helen felt sorry for us so Helen would tell my brother and me to meet her outside the Big Apple Bar on 135th Street and Seventh Avenue. We would wait right around the corner off Seventh Avenue so that no one would see us. Helen would give each of us $2 for lunch. I was so grateful for those two dollars. Back then, $2 got me a Mammy Jammy for a dollar, a soda for 50 cents, and a Suzi Q chocolate cake for 50 cents. I loved Suzy Qs because you got two big cakes. I loved sweets, and Suzy Qs was just enough sweet stuff for me. Other times, Helen would order us some chicken wings from the chicken spot on 135th Street between Seventh and Eighth Avenue. Helen saved me from being hungry plenty of days.

I felt like it was safe to ask Helen if she would be my foster mother. Helen never had foster children before, and she was not licensed to be a foster mother. I would be the first and only foster child she ever took care of but, in order for me to live in Helen's home, she would have to become a licensed foster mother. Helen agreed to become my foster mother and she did not mind going through the process of becoming a foster parent. Becoming a foster mother is a long invasive process. It required letting the Bureau of Child Welfare agency all into your business, such as background checks, medical info, and information about everyone who lived in the household. It was a lot and I appreciated that Helen agreed to go through the process. It meant a lot to me.

My social worker got in touch with Helen and, after everything was confirmed, the process started.

I could not live with Helen until she became licensed so in the mean time I was temporarily placed in a foster home in Jamaica Queens until Helen became a licensed foster parent by BCW.

Jamaica, Queens was cool; I lived in a foster home off of Merrick Boulevard and Lesley Rd. I lived with Mr. and Mrs. Moss, their twin daughters Nita and Quita and a little baby girl. I can't remember her name but I know she was a foster child. The Moss family owned a little grocery store that was connected to their house. The entrance to the store was right on the corner of Merrick Boulevard and Lesley Rd.

Nita and Quita were about 5 years younger than me and the little girl was about 18 months, I was 15. Nita and Quita wore glasses like me, they had jerri curls, and cute faces. They looked alike but I wouldn't say they were identical twins. They liked me and I liked them. I believe that they kind of dug that I was their big sister. Mr. Moss didn't say much, he always took care of the store making sure the grocery stock was good. Mrs. Moss also took care of the store. We used to go to Jetro Wholesale Store to buy products to restock the shelves in the grocery store. Nita, Quita and I worked in the grocery store. I loved going to Jetro Food Wholesale with Mrs. Moss and I loved working in the grocery store. It was a good learning experience living with a family that owned a grocery store.

I went to Andrew Jackson High School because Mrs. Moss' sister-in-law, Mrs. Jackson, worked at Andrew Jackson High School. I believe she was a guidance counselor or the school dean.

Andrew Jackson High was cool. I met a few friends in Andrew Jackson, mostly guys. I don't remember all of their names but I do remember a guy named Wise, and a girl named "Tawanna or Tawanda." I remember Wise because we used to talk a lot. Wise was dark skinned, had a handsome face and nicely built. He was 5 percent Muslim and he used to teach me about his beliefs. Wise and I would have lunch together and sometimes when I went to Harlem on the weekends he would ride with me on the bus to the Jamaica train station. We would talk for a while before I got on the long train ride to Harlem. I liked talking to guys when I was younger. Their conversation was just different and interesting. Girls gossiped too much and I never cared about other people and never got the pleasure out of talking about others in a bad way.

I remember Tawana because I remember going to her house and there were a whole bunch of girls at Tawana house when I went there. I think we were going out to a party or something. I'm not sure but I remember whatever we were doing we had fun. Tawana was brown skin like a pecan brown, slim and seemed to be a social butterfly but very tough. I liked Tawana. I always felt comfortable and safe even if I was doing something wrong, like sneaking to a party.

Mr. and Mrs. Moss were nice to me. I don't remember either of them doing anything wrong to me. I was always treated with respect when I lived with the Moss's. The only thing I did not like about living with Mrs. Moss was that she always wanted to buy me clothes out of the thrift store. Mrs. Moss didn't care about dressing at all. Mr. and Mrs. Moss reminded me of a cowboy and cowgirl for some reason. Maybe Mr. Moss wore a cowboy hat, I can't remember. All I know is shopping at the thrift store for me was a no no. I was young and I knew Mrs. Moss was receiving money to take care of me. So I would get upset and question

Mrs. Moss about buying my clothes from the thrift store. I wanted brand new clothes. I did not want old and used clothes from some thrift store. I gave Mrs. Moss a hard time when it came to buying my clothes. If I knew how much money the agency gave for clothing allowance back then I probably would have shut my mouth. Then again, I didn't care if I spent all my money on one item. I'd rather have one item that I wanted or nothing at all.

Queens was kind of fun and I liked going to Andrew Jackson. The lunchroom in Jackson was always alive with guys doing beats on the lunch room tables, rapping and spitting lyrics to the beats. But it still didn't stop me from wanting to live in Harlem. Harlem was where I was born and raised. Harlem was better to me. Although I could not live with my potential foster mother at the time, I was still able to stay with her on the weekends. every weekend I would get on the train and go to Harlem. I had to take one bus, three different trains and then walk about three blocks. The commute to Harlem always took at least one hour and a half and the same coming back to Queens.

I could not wait to move to Harlem.

HE CHOSE ME

I met Richard over the phone when he was on Rikers Island doing a year bit for a gun charge. And, when he came home, we met face to face by a coincidence.

Helen got her license to become my foster mother around the beginning of 1986. I was fifteen going on sixteen and I was in the eleventh grade. It was perfect timing because the second half of the school year was just getting started and it made my transition from Andrew Jackson to Julia Richmond High school pretty easy. There was no way I was going to continue to go to Andrew Jackson High School and live in Harlem; the commute was just too far. It was also good because I didn't have to worry about losing any class credits because the semester had just started.

I was so happy that I was permanently living with Helen, Yvette and Netta. Living with Helen was happy. Yvette and Netta were both popping and popular. Even though Netta was much quieter and calmer than Yvette, she was still popular. Netta was tall, slim with a nice shape. She was a dancer so she had a gap between her legs and a bridge underneath her ass cheeks. Netta danced her ass off. I loved to see her break dance, every move seemed so smooth and neat. Netta was conservative and preserved. Yvette was different, she was just the opposite. Don't get me wrong, Netta and Yvette both were pretty and they both had nice shapes but when it came to their personalities it was like night and day. Yvette was loud, out spoken and she loved to be the center of attention. Yvette always looked out for her friends but, if you didn't do what she wanted you to do, then you were on her bad side. Most of Yvette's friends were scared of her, in my opinion. I know I was scared. Helen always took up for Yvette, even if Yvette was wrong, she would say, "You know how Yvette is." Netta would get upset and tell Helen she was unfair.

Helen was different from Mary; she let us go outside. Helen wanted us to have fun, when we had fun, she had fun. As long as the house was clean when she came home from work, we could enjoy all the festivities that went on back then. Helen let us go to the Roof Top on Saturday nights and afterward we would stop at Willie Burgers or Sherman's BBQ spot on 145th and 7th Avenue. We always made sure to call home to see if Helen wanted something to eat, that was routine. Every Wednesday we went to see ShowTime at the Apollo with Steve Harvey. Helen let us go out on dates as long as she met the guys; it was usually ok. We went to all the basketball tournaments on 145th Street and at the Rucker Park on 155th Street and 8th Avenue. Living with Helen was exciting and I was happy.

When I first moved back with Helen I used to hang out with Yvette all the time. Netta really didn't hang out, she spent a lot of time with her guy friend. But I loved hanging out with Yvette. We went all over Harlem visiting Yvette's friends and to check out the guys. I remember riding the bikes downtown. We had Ross bikes and we rode our bikes all over. Yvette had beef with girls from all over so, as we rode by certain blocks and housing projects, girls would be grilling us. I didn't know why

Yvette had problems with other females most of the time but I'm sure Yvette had an idea of why. We got into a few fights with females. Back then fighting was fun for me. I didn't start trouble but when someone bothered me, they got it. Yvette and Netta were the same way and whenever somebody fucked with one of us, they had to fuck with all three of us. We had a fight at the Roof Top with some girls from foster projects. One year we were at Virginia Beach for Labor Day walking on the boardwalk One of us got into an altercation with a guy on the boardwalk. I forget the details, but I remember all three of us throwing our hands up to fight at the same time. The guy said, "Dam" y'all don't play" and backed off.

Yvette started dating Richard's cousin Daniel right around the time I started living with them. Daniel was a drug dealer who worked on 145th Street between Seventh and Eighth Avenue inside the Juke Box. The Juke Box was a drug spot disguised as a game room. I knew it was a drug spot because I was dating Daniel's friend Boo and Boo worked inside the Juke Box too. Boo was about five years older than me. He was brown skin, tall and a little husky. He wasn't really my type but he was nice and I liked the things he did for me. He treated me like a cub and always showed me love. I was small and he was kinda big, not fat, but his body frame was at least five times bigger than my body frame. Boo got paid a thousand dollars a week and he would spend most of it with me. He and I would go shopping at VIM, an urban clothing store that sold sneakers and jeans. The store was on 96th Street and Broadway. We would hit the Gap and Foot Locker afterward. Whatever I wanted, he got it for me. After shopping, we would go get something to eat from Dallas BBQ on 72nd Street between Central Park West and Columbus Avenue. Sometimes we went to the steakhouse on 86th Street and other times we went up to Copeland's, a soul food restaurant on 145th. We were always out having fun whenever he was off from work. Boo worked in the Juke Box like it was a nine to five. He worked the second shift four to midnight, Monday thru Saturday and every Saturday night he got paid. Sometimes I would sit in the Juke Box with Boo waiting for him to get off, that's how I know for sure the Juke Box was a drug spot. I'm not sure what Boo's title was but he always seemed to be the man in charge whenever I was there. Every time a customer came through the door they would see Boo first to pay for their drugs. I'm not sure if it was dope, coke, or crack they sold. One thing for sure was they all looked like drug addicts.

Daniel started coming to see Yvette all the time. Sometimes, Boo was with him and sometimes he wasn't . Since Daniel spent a lot of time at our house with Yvette, he gave Richard the phone number to the crib. Richard and Daniel were first cousins, their mothers were sisters. It was important to Daniel that Richard was always able to contact him. I'm not sure if the phone calls were business or personal but one thing for sure, Daniel was always there when Richard called.

One day I answered the house phone, and the operator said, "You have a collect call from an inmate by the name of 'Rich' from Rikers Correctional Facility. Press 'one' to accept, or press 'two' to hang up." I pressed "one" and accepted the call. At this time the inmates had to make collect calls, meaning the receiver would be charged for the phone call. In Richard's case I knew it was okay to accept the call because Richard always called Helen's house to speak to Daniel. This was not the first time I answered the phone and Richard was on the other end. Besides, Daniel was hustling in the streets; he had money to pay the phone bill if needed.

Back then, guys that hustled never hesitated to pay a phone bill or any bill and we never hesitated to let them use our phone if needed. Now if you didn't have shit to offer, meaning no money to pay a phone bill then no we were not letting you run our bills up.

Men and women were different back then. I grew up around men that were providers. The women that raised me all dealt with men that owned buildings, funeral parlors, laundromats, candy stores, restaurants, meat markets, florist shops, game rooms, pool halls, number spots and some of them were in the drug game. They knew how to treat a woman. Men back then had too much pride to be in a female's face if they did not have a dime and could not provide. On the other hand, the women I grew up with took care of the men. They ironed their clothes, prepared dinner, set the table, took a bath every night and they went to bed looking nice. All I have to say is that things have changed.

Anyway, I said, "Hello." He said, "Hello." I said, "Hold on, let me get Daniel." Rich asked, "Is this Angie?" I answered, "Yes, this is Angela." "Wait a minute let me talk to you." "Me?" "Yeah you. I heard about you." "What you heard about me?" I asked. "I heard you was a good girl," he answered. "What's a good girl?" I replied. "You. You're a good girl," he repeated. I didn't know what he meant by a "good girl," and I was thinking, What's a 'good girl' because I ain't no virgin. I laugh now, because I now know being a "good girl" had nothing to do with being a virgin. "Nah, your brother Raymond told me you was a good girl." Raymond was from the block, 142nd Street; we grew up together and he called me his little sister. Raymond and Richard did time together on the Island.

I probably talked to Richard for about two minutes before I told Daniel to come get the phone. I don't remember what I said but I know our conversation was short. Honestly I don't really remember talking to

Richard on the phone a lot at all after that. I had Boo, I didn't know who Richard was and I just wasn't interested. I didn't even know Richard was home from jail until I saw him by a coincidence.

One day, I was walking across 141st Street on Lenox Avenue in Harlem. I was on my way to Helen's house. A gray Saab was at the light. As I walked across 141st Street, the person in the gray Saab beeped the horn. I looked to my left and from the corner of my eye, I could see that only the driver was in the car. I couldn't see clearly because the vision in my left eye is limited but I could tell it was a guy; he was dark chocolate with a bald head. I didn't get a good look at his face. It was a quick glance and I couldn't really see. I didn't wanna make it obvious that I was looking at him, so I did not look for long. I didn't want him to think, for one second, I approved of his car-honking tactic. Honestly, I always hated the car horn honking shit. It annoyed me.

As soon as I stepped foot on the sidewalk, the number runners and the older men that sat on the corner said, "That's right, keep walking, don't pay them horns no attention." I always respected older people. Their approval meant a lot to me. And the fact that I never liked the horn blowing thing didn't help much. I kept walking, looking straight, and never turned my head. I really didn't care.

A few days later Yvette and I were coming from the laundromat. It was spring of 1986. The weather was nice, it was a Saturday afternoon, right around noon time. Yvette and I had got up early to go do the laundry and we were on our way back home. We both had a shopping cart full of clothes. We always had a lot of clothes to wash. Back then nobody liked going out to the laundromat. There were a lot of times we would just go buy an outfit to wear instead of doing laundry so by the time we did laundry it was a whole lot of clothes to wash.

Yvette and I were walking down the block pushing our shopping carts. I forget what Yvette had on but I remember I had on some sweatpants, a tee shirt and I had a scarf on my head. I definitely remember that part. That's why I truly believe if a man likes you, he likes you. It's not about how cute you are or how big your butt is. Love comes from the heart and God has to play a part.

We were halfway down the block, and I heard the song Fools Paradise by Melissa Morgan. The music was coming from a car driving down the block. The music was loud but the stereo system was good, so it was ok, besides Fools Paradise was one of my favorite songs back then.

It looked like the same gray car that was beeping at me the other day when I was crossing 141st Street. The car passed by us, pulled over and a guy got out of the car. Yvette immediately said, "What's up cuz!?" She seemed really excited to see him. In my mind, I was saying, "This must be the same guy that was beeping his horn at me when I was crossing 141st Street." It looked like the same car.

It was the same guy; I could tell by the shape of his head and the color of his skin. It was the same big-boxed head that I saw when I glanced through the front window of the car that was blowing the horn at me.

Richard looked at me, his eyes made contact with mine.

Richard asked Yvette, "Is this Angie?"

Yvette answered, "Yes, that's Angie, that's my sister."

Richard said, "She played me the other day." I didn't say anything at first, I just stayed quiet as he looked me up and down.

"Why did you play me like that?" he asked.

"What do you mean, why I played you? I didn't play you. You beeped the horn at me—did I look like a hooker to you?" I replied.

Richard stood back on his legs and said, "Oh, so you have a smart mouth. I apologize, I didn't mean to offend you."

"I'm just playing with you. But I really don't do horns," I said.

He replied, "I get that Ang. Is it okay for me to call you Ang?"

"Yeah, you can call me Ang, I like the name Ang," I said.

"Let's go out and get something to eat later—beep me," he passed me a piece of paper with his beeper number on it.

I smiled and said, "I have a boyfriend."

Richard immediately did a little chuckle and said, "And what your man have to do with me?"

We both laughed and I said, "I'll beep you later and let you know when we can go out." Richard got back in his car and drove off.

I never asked Richard his name and he did not put his name on the piece of paper with his beeper number. Yvette called him cuz so I assumed that was Richard, Daniel's cousin. She and I continued to walk down the block. As we walked down the block, I asked her if that was Richard, and she said it was. I thought, Wait a minute, you mean to tell me that's the same Richard I've been talking to on the phone all this time? He's the same guy that's been calling the house to speak to Daniel. That's crazy that we never saw each other and it just so happened to be me that he was beeping the horn at. What a coincidence. That's was what I thought then but now I know it was not a coincidence. It was divine and intentional through the grace of God. "Yes, that's Richard

Porter!" she said.

"He ain't that cute, so what is the big deal?" I asked Yvette.

Yvette said, "Rich is the man, ask anybody in Harlem."

I stayed quiet and continued pushing the shopping cart down the block to the building.

I was putting away my clothes when Richard called. It was less than an hour from the time that I got home from the laundromat. "What are you doing?" he asked. "I'm putting away my clothes, listening to music and chilling," I answered. "Why, what's up with you?" "When you gonna let me take you out?" Richard asked. "I don't know, soon, I promise," I said.

Richard called me every day. He called every day to see if I was ready to go out with him. He was very persistent. Finally, one day I told him he could take me out. We both agreed to go out to eat on the following Friday. Fridays were good for me, because my boyfriend didn't get off from work until midnight so Friday was perfect for me. So, I agreed we'd go out on Friday.

Our first date was amazing. He called me around 5 o'clock to tell me to be ready at 7:00pm because he was coming to pick me up. I was 16 years old and still underage, so I asked my foster mother if it was okay. I had already asked her earlier in the week, so she knew I was going out with Richard. I just needed to remind her and tell her the time frame I would be gone. I remember when I first told her I was going on a date with Richard, she jokingly said she was going to tell my boyfriend. We laughed, and I left her room so excited that she said yes.

7 o'clock came and the phone rang. It was Richard. "Are you ready?" he asked. "Yes," I responded. "Look out the window," he said. I put the phone down on the kitchen counter and went to look out of the kitchen window. The kitchen window was able to go up high, so I was able to stick my head out of the window over the window guards. When I opened up the window and stuck my head out, Richard was looking up with roses in one hand and a little cute teddy bear in his arm. I smiled so hard. "I'm coming down," I said.

As soon as I hit the bottom of the steps in my building, I could see Richard standing in front of the building. He saw me coming out of the building through the glass doors and stepped up and opened the door to the building. As I walked out of the building, I could not help but notice how sharp he was. His hair was cut and he had on some Diadora sneakers with some blue jeans and a Polo shirt. He smelled so good. I think he had on some cologne by Pierre Cardin, I don't quite remember. But I can't forget how good he smelled. Richard opened the door to the building and said, "Hey Ang, what's up?" "Hey Rich, what's up," I replied with a smile on my face. Not too big and not too small, but a smile that was in between. He walked me to his car. A Saab 900 Turbo. It was a gray stone color, shiny and clean. He opened the door for me, I got in, and he closed the door behind me. As he walked past the front of the car, I thought, "What a gentleman."

Richard never asked or told me where we were going. "How was your day? How was school?" he asked. "My day was good. School was fine." I was very quiet and did not say much. We pulled up in front of this burger spot. It was Jackson Hole. Jackson Hole was a popping burger spot. There were a few Jackson Holes in the city but we went to the Jackson Hole on Third Avenue in Manhattan around 86th Street.

We were able to park right across the street in front of a meter. Rich got out of the car, paid the meter, came back to the car and opened the door for me. As soon as I got out of the car, he took my hand and we walked to the restaurant. During dinner we laughed, joked, and shared some of our dreams. He told me he wanted to be a basketball player and I shared with him that I wanted to be a model and actress.

"So why are you living in a foster home? Where's your mom?" Richard asked me. I told him that my mom had died a few years ago and I had been living in foster care since I was about five years old.

I explained to Richard that my mother was addicted to heroin. I told him someone called the Bureau of Child Welfare on my mom because she used to leave us in the house by ourselves. My siblings and I were put into foster care, and we never got the chance to live back with our mother again because she died. We stayed with my mother on the weekends. She had just gotten clean from using heroin. She was in the process of getting us back when she died.

Richard asked me how was it living in foster homes. I told him I didn't like it. The home I was in at the time was okay, but other homes that I lived in were very strict. There was a lot of discipline but no love. Me and my siblings use to get our asses whopped with the extension cord all the time when I lived with Mary. I got beat for shit my siblings did. They used to steal Mary's money all the time. No one confessed to stealing her money. So we all got beat.

"Yeah, I used to get my ass whoop to. You're not the only one that got beat with an extension cord, I got my ass whoop a few times with an extension cord. A lot of black parents in the hood whooped their children's asses with extension cords" Richard said. "Well I'm not going to beat my children. I don't believe beating children, screaming and calling them names is beneficial." "Yeah me neither. I don't want no one beating or mistreating my children."

"My worst experience was living with Mary," I said. "My siblings always felt like Mary treated me better. It wasn't that she treated me better. I believe Mary trusted me because I didn't tell lies or steal. Whenever she wanted to know something she would always say to me, 'Come here, come right here, stand right in front of me, I'm to find out the truth right now.' She just knew I was going to tell. And honestly if I knew the answer most likely I was telling. Mary would make me stand right in front of her. Then she would say, 'I'm going to ask you one time and you better tell me the truth.' I would be so scared. Mary made me stand in front of her like she always did. 'Who stole my money? ' she asked me. I didn't want to tell on my brother but I was scared to lie. I stood in front of Mary and in my mind I was talking to God. I took too long to answer and the next thing I knew I was seeing colors. Mary slapped the shit out of me. After that slap I hurried up and told on my brother. I was crying and holding my face. " Donald had a hundred dollar bill today," I said. "Dam so you was a tattle teller?" Richard asked. I didn't want to tell him I was scared to lie. "I hated living there, sometimes Mary made me stay up all night scratching her hair or scraping her feet with a knife. "Get the comb and come scratch my hair.' If it wasn't the comb then she was telling me to get the bucket and knife out of the kitchen to do her feet. She would send everyone else to bed. I believe my siblings saw this as a privilege, but it wasn't, to me it was more like torture. Yo, I use to be so sleepy. One time I fell asleep scratching her hair in the same spot. She screamed so loud. 'You retarded bitch if you dig in my fucking head one more time I'm going to beat the shit out of you.' I couldn't even keep my eyes open. I was so happy when she told me to go to bed." Richard was like "Dam that's fucked up". "Yeah I remember one time I drank water out of the toilet because I was thirsty. I was scared to cut the faucet on because I didn't want to get in trouble and I would not dare open the refrigerator. We were only allowed to go in the refrigerator."

Well that's nasty." "The toilet was clean." "Nah I'm just playing That's fucked up that you had to do that." "Yeah, foster care has not been a good experience. I lived with Mary's sister Lolo. She was a licensed foster mother also. Well Aunty Lolo was crazy too, she used to put shit in the milk to make you shit. She wanted to catch who was drinking the milk at night so she put some sort of stool relaxer in the milk. My brother was also living with Lolo at the time. And he was the culprit. That milk had my brother shitting all day."

"Dam. I'm sorry you had to go through all of that, Richard said. I told him that it was okay and I had started running away when I turned 14.

I explained to him why I ran away so much. I told him I decided that I would run away from any home that I did not like after my mother died. I would rather have no guardian than stay in a home where they beat me and called me names all day. I hated when my previous foster family or anyone called me retarded.

"Yeah my mom is addicted to heroin too. My father got clean a few years ago, so I know how you feel," Richard assured me. "Some days I be so upset at my moms, but I love her," he continued. "Thank God she is still here."

"I don't care if my mom was addicted to heroin, I just wish she was still here with me," I said. I asked Richard did he have any other siblings.

He told me he had a few sisters and one little brother. "I take care of my little brother Donnell, he's eight years old. My little brother is my world. I have to look out for him. I make sure he goes to school and has everything he needs to succeed."

"So what school do you go to?" "I go to Julia Richmond on 68th Street." "Yeah I know where Richmond is. I went to Martin Luther King but I dropped out. School is over for me. I'm twenty years old, I'm not thinking about going back to school. My goal is to own property, land, and some businesses. I'm thinking about opening up a laundromat. I'm not sure right now but I'm definitely going to start a business. I have plans to buy land somewhere, I just haven't figured out, what state I wanna buy land in. I don't want to stay in New York City all of my life, I know that for sure.

"So what about you? What do you wanna do with your life?" Richard asked. "Well of course finish high school and then go to college. I want to be a nurse." Every time someone asked me what I wanted to be I would say, "I want to be a nurse." Clearly, I didn't know myself because I know there was no way I could have ever been a nurse. I can't stand to see blood and, honestly, I would never be able to stick a needle in anyone.

"A nurse that's cool, I always wanted to be an NBA player." "For real?" "Yeah I think basketball players are cool and they make a lot of money. I know one thing, I never wanted to and I never want to work for anyone. I plan on being my own boss always. There's a lot of ways to make money. Ever since I was younger, I've been hustling. It all started with me getting the newspaper on Sundays for the older people in my grandmother's building on 132nd Street. They would give me two dollars to get the Sunday newspaper from the news stand. The paper cost a dollar fifty and they told me to keep the change. The more people I got the Sunday newspaper for the more money I made. I started knocking on doors asking all the neighbors in the building if they wanted me to get the Sunday newspaper. During the week after school and on the weekends in the morning I used to pack bags. All the cashiers wanted me on their line because I packed the bags neatly and I didn't waste time. I was the fastest packer in the store. I didn't waste time because that was my money. Every time I packed a bag the customer would give me a tip, a quarter, 50 cents and sometimes a dollar. The more bags I packed the more money I made. At the end of the week, I would have at least $100. That's how I stayed fresh and brought the sneakers and clothes I wanted. My mother wasn't able to give me what I wanted so I learned ways to make money on my own. Once you understand supply and demand all you have to do is figure the needs out, Ang. The needs are the opportunities and everyone needs are based on their lifestyle.

"So do you have any children?" Richard answered "No I don't have any children." "There's a female who had a son. She tried to say that I'm her son's father but I don't think so. We were supposed to do a court order paternity test but she never showed up in court". "Wwhat happened after that?" "She moved some place and I haven't heard or seen her since then. Why? Are you gonna have my baby?" "Stop playing. I'm not having no baby no time soon. The foster homes I grew up in were tough and I'm not having children until I am sure I can take care of them. I never want my children to ever have to live with anyone else but me." "Yo, I understand you and I feel the same way. I wanna make sure my children's life is different from mine. I wanna make sure I'm able to provide my children with the tools they need to survive in life.

"Yo, I could talk to you all night long." When Richard said that I just smiled. I knew right away I was comfortable. I didn't talk a whole lot that night but I talked enough and it was more than normal for me.

"Come on let's get out of here and get you home before you get in trouble." "In trouble from who?" "You know. Don't your boyfriend Boo get off soon?" "So I see you like being sarcastic?" "Nah I'm not being sarcastic, I just don't want you to get into any trouble." "I can't get in trouble because he my boyfriend not my husband or my father."

The waitress stopped at our table, "Is there anything else I can get for you two?" "You want something else?" "No, I'm good." "Nah we good, you can bring the check."

The waitress came back and handed him the check. As the waitress was about to go away, Richard said, "Hold up." He took a knot of money out of his pocket, peeled off some bills, gave the waitress the money and said, "No change. Thank you."

As soon as we stepped out of Jackson Hole, Richard took my hand. We walked along Third Avenue until we got to the light then crossed the street to get to his car. He opened the car door for me. I thanked him and he stared into my eyes and said, "You are welcome" as he shut the car door.

We drove up Third Avenue until we reached 115th Street, then we made a left and went straight up to 7th Avenue. Once we hit 7th Avenue, we made a right, going uptown, that was when I became alert because now we were on my side of town, Central Harlem. I never knew a lot people but a lot of people knew me and I did not want to be seen.

The sky was clear, and the weather was so perfect, not too hot, and not too cold, it was just right. It was a beautiful spring night.

When we got back to 142nd Street, Richard and I sat in the car in front of my building talking. The windows were down, and the music was low. Richard noticed my boyfriend coming to the car through his rearview mirror. "Yo, your man is coming." I said, "Oh my God." "Don't worry I got you," Richard said. Boo walked up to the car, Richard rolled the window up and made sure the doors were locked. Boo reached to touch the car door and Richard gave him a look like, "Get the fuck away from my car." Boo backed away from the car and Richard pulled off. Richard made a right at the light. We drove down Lenox Avenue and Richard made another right at 139th Street. He pulled over on 139th Street between 7th and 8th Avenues. We talked for a while, and then he took me home.

When I got back to my block, Boo was not downstairs but he was upstairs inside of the house crying to Helen. I told him it was just a date, and I didn't mean to hurt his feelings. "I know Rich is going to take you from me. I know he is," that's all Boo kept saying. Boo knew whose car I was in, so he already knew who Richard was. Every drug dealer in Harlem knew who Richard was, besides Boo hung out with Richard's cousin Daniel. "It was just a date, that doesn't mean that I'm going to leave you for him," I said. "I can't compete with Rich, you can be with him." Boo said goodnight and that was the end of our relationship.

I introduced Richard to Helen, and she was okay with me dating him. Helen knew Richard was the reason why Boo and I broke up and Helen also knew a little about Richard from Yvette and Netta. And she knew that Richard and Daniel were cousins. Helen let me go out on dates with Richard and that was the beginning of history.

WHO THE HELL IS RICH PORTER

ord got around Harlem fast that I was dating Richard. I really didn't understand how so many people were in my business so fast, well—our business, it was crazy. I guess I didn't realize how much of a hot topic Richard was. Or maybe I didn't realize how much everyone talked in the hood. I was very humble, quiet, and it's okay to say, I was naive back then. A lot of shit went on in Harlem that I didn't understand and most of the time it went right over my head. I guess some people would say I didn't have common sense but I would say, no, I just didn't have much in common with most people from Harlem. I was different.

I went out with Richard on Friday, and by Monday morning, our relationship was the headline of Harlem.

I walked out of my building to go to school. The sun was vibrant and so was the smile on my face. I had been speaking to Richard all weekend after our amazing date and I was feeling great. When I got to the corner of 142nd Street and Lenox Avenue, some of the guys from the block were standing in front of the bodega. My block was always lit, even early in the morning. The guys would be out standing in front of the bodega joking, dealing, or just chilling. All eyes were on me. I said, "Well, what y'all looking at?" They were looking at me like I hit the lottery or something. "Yeah Ang, you fucking with RP," one guy said. "Who the fuck is RP?" I asked. Another guy said, "Rich, Richie Rich. Yo Ang, you fucking with one of the top niggas in Harlem."

My bus was coming so I started walking away toward the bus stop. As I walked away, I said, "No, Richie Rich is fucking with the top chick." I was always very quiet on the outside yet very confident on the inside. Guys on my block always played with me. They would always call me ugly. I would simply say, "Stop playing, 'cause the mirror don't lie." Sometimes, guys would call me conceited, but I was just confidently convinced that I was beautiful, and they helped convince me.

I got on the M102 bus and headed to school. My friend Shia got on the bus at 140th Street and Lenox Avenue. Shia lived on 140th Street between Lenox and 7th Avenue. I met Shia on the bus in 1984 when I first started going to Julia Richmond, when I was in the ninth grade. Shia sat next to me, and as soon as her ass hit the seat, she asked me about Richard. She seemed to be more excited that I was going out with Richard than I was. I wondered, "Damn, bitch, how did you know that I went on a date with Richard? Anyway. Who the hell is Richard Porter?" She told me that everyone knows Rich Porter. I asked, "Well how come I don't know him?" and we laughed and went to school.

Richard started coming to pick me up from my block all the time. And every time he picked me up it was like a movie scene. I didn't understand it and honestly I had never seen the streets give one man so much love and attention. Richard could be picking me up from my block, from my school or just be driving by, it didn't matter he was always seen.

When he came to pick me up, by the time I got downstairs Richard would be out of his car standing back on his legs talking to a few guys from around my way. Richard always seemed to be comfortable whenever he was around 142nd Street. He laughed, joked, and showed off; he was always a very proud man. He loved the way people admired his cars, clothes, jewelry, and most importantly he loved when they listened to what he had to say.

Richard was smart, he kept up with current events, finance, and new technologies. He was able to have a conversation with anybody and he loved sharing his knowledge. It was not odd to catch Richard sitting in his car reading the newspaper.

Richard and I were not dating long before he started coming to pick me up from school. That's when I realized he was known all over the city. The first time he picked me up from school it was a surprise, I didn't know he was coming.

School was over and I came out of the 68th Street entrance, 68th and 2nd Ave. Richard was sitting diagonally across the street from the entrance in his Wrangler Jeep. I noticed Richard and he noticed me.

Guys and girls from Queens, Brooklyn, and the Bronx were all standing around watching. I was aware of all the attention Richard got but I never really processed how serious it was.

I walked over to Richard's car, the front seat was empty, for me. I got in the car, Alpo and Azie sitting in the back. I said hello, they both said hello back. I didn't really know Azie or Alpo. I had seen both of them coming and going whenever I went to see Boo, my old boyfriend, at the

Juke Box but I didn't know them. I remember running into Alpo one time before I ever knew of Richard Porter. It was when I was on one of my run away missions. Actually it was when I left the dude's apartment that almost got robbed on Bradhurst Avenue. I was walking downtown from 149th Street on Eighth Avenue. When I got to 145th Street I turned to go to Seventh Avenue, walking on the opposite side of the Juke Box. Alpo was standing in front of a building on the same side I was walking on. The building was not too far from the corner of Seventh Avenue. Alpo said, "Come here." I started speed walking until I got around the corner. It was something about his spirit that scared me. I never spoke to Alpo until he started being with Richard. Richard got in the car, and we sat there for about ten minutes while they looked at girls until Azie and Alpo started being disrespectful.

I didn't agree with the way Azie or Alpo were talking about females. I'm a female and I was not going to sit there and tolerate the disrespect. Besides, one of the females that Alpo was talking about was a female that I knew from around my neighborhood. Alpo spotted her standing in front of Julia Richmond High school. He said, "That's a begging bitch right there." I forget what I said exactly, but I believe I said something like, "Don't talk about females like that. Yo don't talk like that around her. Don't curse, don't do none of the dumb shit." Then Richard said, "She's different, she's a good girl," and Alpo and Azie both shut up.

Alpo was always disrespectful when it came to females. I always said you had to be a certain type of female to fuck with Alpo. I didn't know too much about Azie because Richard spent more time with Alpo.

There were plenty of times that Richard came and picked me up from school. But that was the last and only time I ever remember him picking me up with Azie and Alpo in the car.

Now, there were times when we would meet Alpo somewhere. Like the time we met Alpo at the car dealership in New Jersey. Richard was buying his BMW. We met Alpo in Jersey at the BMW dealer. Right in Teaneck. The car dealer was so happy to see Richard. He showed Richard the 325i and Richard was excited like a little kid. "Test it out," the car dealer said. "Ang, get in." I got in the car and we drove around the block. When we got back to the dealership. Richard let the car dealer know he wanted the car, "I like the car, it drives nice." Richard went to his car, popped the trunk, and took out a shoe box. Richard got in the car, opened up the shoe box, and took out four stacks of twenty-dollar bills wrapped in rubber bands. Richard handed me two stacks and told me to count it and make sure there was $5,000 in each stack. We both counted two stacks each and made sure each stack had $5,000. He took the two stacks from me, put them with the two stacks he had, put the top of the shoe box back on and put the box in the back seat. He said, "I'll be right back, let me just give them this money for the car."

Alpo was already there dealing with another salesperson. I remember because Alpo was fucking with me on this day. He was fucking with me because I had just totaled a car.

It was Helen's boyfriend's daughter's car. I was driving without a license and I didn't know how to drive. I was turning the corner on 142nd Street and Seventh Avenue and I lost control of the car. I was going too fast and didn't know that I needed to slow down. The car went into the iron gates in front of the building on the corner and the car was totaled. Thank God no one got hurt.

After Richard and Alpo was finished at the BMW dealership, we went to this popular hoagie spot in Teaneck to get a hoagie sandwich. Richard loved their turkey and cheese. He always liked for them to put

French dressing on his sandwich. Richard was not a Hellman's person, he liked miracle whip and so did I. Miracle Whip was sweet and so was french dressing. It made sense for Richard to like french dressing on his sandwiches. It was mid day, around three pm, the parking lot at the hoagie spot was empty, so Richard let me practice driving in his car. Honestly, I forget what car it was but I do remember Alpo laughing, joking, and screaming out loud to watch out. I drove a little bit without hurting myself or anyone else, but I was really scared to drive after I totaled the car.

Sometimes when Richard picked me up from school, I would ask him if my friends could come and he would say yes. We had so much fun especially when the weather was nice. Richard would take us to City Island to Shelton's and sometimes we would go all the way to Great Adventure Amusement Park in New Jersey.

A lot of times Richard picked me up after school and it would be just me and him. We went on shopping sprees and out to eat.

I didn't have to ask Richard for anything because he always made sure I was straight. He gave me money, brought me jewelry, and he loved taking me clothes shopping.

Richard always made sure I had money. Whenever he saw me he gave me at least two hundred dollars. I was only sixteen and back then two hundred dollars to spend on whatever was a lot. I probably could have had a lot of shit but I wasn't that chick. I never cared about material things. I was more interested in having fun with my friends than spending my money on a bunch of Gucci bags. Honestly, I didn't know a lot about designer brands. I knew about Gucci and Louis Vuitton but they were for the grown folks not the kids back then. I was young without any real guidance, so I didn't think to save shit up and there was no one to advise me. I was always very generous and giving. When you grow up in foster care, it becomes a habit to compromise and share. It can be a good thing but I've learned it can be a disservice to myself and others if I'm not aware. Whenever Richard gave me money it went in one hand and out the other because I always shared with my friend. Richard didn't care about me spending my money fast, by then he had realized what type of female I was, so whenever he saw me, he would put more money in my pockets. He wanted me to be able to go to the movies, skating, and out to eat if I wanted to. Richard never wanted me just sitting outside or walking the streets doing nothing.

One day in the summer of 1986 I was standing around my girlfriend's block on 144th Street. Richard drove down the block and saw me standing there. It was dark outside and Richard was on his way home. Richard pulled over and I got in the car. "Yo what are you doing standing out here?" "I'm waiting on my friend, she went upstairs to see her boyfriend real quick." "And she left you down here?" "Yeah she should be back soon." "When she comes back what are y'all going to do?" "I don't know." "What do you mean you don't know?" Richard reached into his pocket, and he gave me two hundred dollar bills. "Here take this. Y'all go get something to eat or do something. I don't want you walking the streets. Only hoes walk the streets." My friend walked up, I got out of the car, Richard drove off and we caught a cab downtown to get something to eat.

When Luther Vandross had a concert in New York City, Richard got a ticket for me and my friend Nia. I met Nia through Shia; Shia and Nia were sisters. Nia was pretty, quiet, and always very classy. Nia had a man that was in the streets so we understood each other's relationship.

Richard knew I loved Luther Vandross. Nia was a fan of Luther's too, actually Nia loved all types of music. Nia and I had become really close and we were always together so Richard got both of us a ticket to see Luther Vandross at Madison Square Garden.

I was excited about going to the concert and I was so happy that Richard got not only me a ticket, but he got a ticket for me to take a friend. I was happy to share the love. Nia said, " Angie stop playing with me, now, you know I wanna go." "Alright the show is at the Garden in this Saturday coming up, at 8pm."

When we got to the show, we were right in the front. We had Orchestra seats and we were in the front row.

GIFTS, FUN, & LOVE

There is sugar and spice that comes with dealing with a man in the drug game. Here's the sugar.

The first pieces of jewelry Richard purchased for me were two pairs of earrings. He picked me up from school and he had a little bag from Macy's. When I got in the car, he gave me the Macy's bag. It had two little boxes. Both boxes had earrings in them. First of all, I was like, "Who buys earrings from Macy's?" Back then, everybody in the city was going to Canal Street for earrings. One box had diamond studs and the other box contained a pair of hoops. Most girls wore hoops back then. They all seemed to be the same. Door knockers, bamboo earrings, or seashells were what most girls wore.

The hoops that Richard bought me were different, they were a design I had never seen on any other female. The earrings were of a better quality than the door knockers you got from Canal Street, and you could tell just by looking at them.

Richard and I had been dating for about four months when his birthday came around. July 26, 1986. I wanted to get Richard something really nice for his birthday. I went down to Canal Street to buy him a piece of jewelry. When I got to Canal Street, I looked in a few jewelry stores for different jewelry for men. I didn't see anything I wanted in my price range. I decided that I was going to buy Richard a nugget bracelet because I ran into this guy that was selling a gold nugget bracelet right outside on Canal Street for what I thought was a good deal.

I was so excited to give Richard his gift. I just knew he would love his new gold nugget bracelet. Richard came upstairs, it was the evening of his birthday. I gave him a birthday card and a gift box with the nugget bracelet in it. Richard opened the card up first. He read it out loud, trying to be funny. Then he opened up the box. Richard took the nugget bracelet out and started to laugh. "Yo where did you get this bracelet from?" I said in a low tone, "I got it from Canal Street." "Did you get it from a store?" "No, this guy was selling it, he said it was 14 carat gold." Richard started to laugh, "Yo he got you, how much money did you give him?" "I gave him one hundred dollars." Richard chuckled and shook his head. "Y'all got rubbing alcohol?" "Yes." "Go put a little in a bowl for me. Let me show you something." I got the rubbing alcohol, put some in the bowl and gave it to Richard. Richard dropped the bracelet inside of the rubbing alcohol. The bracelet immediately turned brown. I wanted to cry. I was so hurt. Richard said, "Don't ever buy anything from anyone off the street again." Not long after that, Richard got us both a nugget bracelet with diamonds.

The jewelry he got for me was always dainty but very high quality, never too big or bulky looking and always lightweight. My diamonds were always pointers, not chips. Most of the time, I had no idea that Richard was buying me a piece of jewelry.

I was working in Helen's soul food restaurant on 7th Avenue between 135th and 136th Street. "Mama's." Helen named the Restaurant Mama's after her mother and her mother was one of the cooks at the restaurant.

I was a waitress at the restaurant. I'll never forget the day Richard brought the ring sizer to the restaurant to get the size of my finger. Richard and Alpo pulled up in front of the restaurant on their motorcycles. They were on the side walk right in front of the restaurant window. Richard never got off of his bike neither did Alpo. I looked at Richard through the window and Richard waved his hand telling me to come outside.

When I got outside Richard asked me for my hand. He took it and measured my finger with a ring sizer. It had a few different rings on it of all different sizes. Richard tried each one until he found my ring size. After he found my ring size, he rode off with Alpo and I went back inside the restaurant to finish working. When Richard checked my ring size, I knew he was buying me a ring. I just didn't know what kind of ring.

About a week later Richard surprised me with a name ring. We went to the hibachi restaurant right off of Route 17 by the Garden State Mall. I went to the bathroom and when I returned to the table, there was a little gift box sitting on my plate. The box was gold, wrapped with a red ribbon and a bow tie on top. I was surprised. "What did you get me?" He told me to open it. Inside was a name ring—a diamond name ring. And the diamonds were pointers, not chips.

Richard loved to take me shopping. It was like he thought I was a baby doll. His favorite department stores were Saks and Bloomingdales and he would have me in both stores trying on item after item. Richard was a bug when it came to clothes and shoes. He loved fashion. I would be in the fitting room already trying on a bunch of items and Richard would still be sending in items for me to try on. "Here give her this," over and over again I would hear Richard giving the sales representatives items for me to try on.

"Let me see Ang, let me see how the clothes look on you." I was kind of shy and I felt a little uncomfortable, but I still showed Richard. Eventually I got comfortable and started modeling the clothes like I was on the runway. Richard would just look at me and smile. After the show was over, Richard and I would decide what items I should keep.

Richard had a love for clothes, but his love was even bigger for sneakers and shoes. Especially sneakers, Richard loved Diadora's and Nike's.

One day in the summer of 1986 Richard took me shopping and he brought me ten pairs of shoes. All of the shoes cost over two hundred dollars. We were walking through the mall and he kept seeing sandals that he wanted me to have. "Yo try these on," over and over again. Some of the shoes were comfortable and some were not. Most of the sandals I wore one time and that was it. Honestly, I've always been a sneaker girl so sandals or shoes was not what I preferred to wear on my feet.

The summer of 1986 was lit, in my eyes it was all about Richard and me. It was my first summer living with Helen. Helen let us be happy, Yvette, Netta and me. And she allowed me to be happy with Richard that summer. We went on dates and we ate at different places. It was the summer when we first had sex.

The way Richard treated me made me want to have sex with him immediately. But Richard felt different, he wanted to wait. There were times that we were making out, and I wanted to give him some, but he was not ready for us to make love yet. I can't remember if I was pushing up on him, or what, but I do recall him telling me that he didn't want me for my sex. "I don't wanna have sex with you yet, I could get sex from any where, I don't want you for your sex, I like you."

So we waited and the more we waited, dated and spent time with each other, the more our love grew for one another. By the time Richard and I had sex, it was so much more than the sex that bonded us together. We shared similar life experiences and we both had the same type of dreams and goals. One goal we both shared was to make sure our children would have a better life than we had. Richard said he loved me and he would always say, "You different Ang, you different, I want you to have my baby."

Richard would always tell his friends that I was different. One time Richard, Alpo and I were in the car together. I can't remember where we were going and I don't remember the exact date but I do know it was in the summer of 1986. We were driving somewhere, I was being quiet as usual. Richard said to Alpo, "This is my baby. She different, she don't care about money and material things, all she wanna do is have fun, she gonna have my baby, she's gonna have my baby."

Richard was different to me too; his love was different. It was genuine, nurturing, and loving. Richard was confident and he took a lot of pride in himself. He was always clean and all of his clothes went to the cleaners except for his underwear. Richard was driven and he a had a vision of a lifestyle he wanted not just for himself but for his wife and his children to come.

The first time Richard and I had sex was at his apartment at the Harmon Cove Towers in Secaucus, New Jersey. After going out to eat at the Hibachi restaurant off Rte 17, we went to his apartment in Harmon Cove. Richard and I had been dating since March or April 1986 and it was July 1986. It was right around Richard's birthday, July 26th 1986, I was seventeen years old. If I'm not mistaken that was the occasion for Richard and I to make love.

It was the first time Richard took me to his apartment in Harmon Cove. When he first came home, he had an apartment in Fort Lee, New Jersey. It was right off of Route 4. I had been there with him, it was where he and I use to count his money. That apartment was not fixed up at all. In fact, I can't remember anything but shoe boxes. Shoe boxes full of money. I'm sure there was probably a couch or a bed there because that's where we kissed and touched, we just never had sex there.

Richard's apartment in Harmon Cove was beautiful. Richard was proud to live in Harmon Cove Towers. Richard even pulled into the parking lot with confidence, it was just something about the way he pressed on the gas, you knew when Richard was pulling in.

Now that I think about it Richard had so much swag. Richard had swag in his fashion, in the way he talked, the way he walked, and he had swag in the way he drove his cars. So Much Swag. SMS.

I remember us walking from the parking garage. We entered the building. The doorman was there. Richard said, "Hey sir, how are you?" The doorman said, "I'm doing great, thank you." We got on the elevator and as soon as the elevator door closed, Richard said, "They love me in this building, they think I'm a basket ball player." I responded and jokingly said, "They don't think you no basketball player, Richard please." "Yes they do, there's a few basketball players that live in here." Richard named a couple of basketball players who lived at Harmon Cove but I can't remember which ones.

Richard opened up the door to his apartment and told me to come inside. As soon as I walked through the door, I took my shoes off. The kitchen was to the right, his bedroom was to the left down the hall, and the dining area and living room was in the middle adjacent to each other.

There were two bathrooms, one in the hallway and the other one was off of Richard's bedroom on the left. Richard's apartment was at least 1000 square feet.

Richard's apartment was decorated tastefully. Not only did Richard take pride in his cars and the way he dressed, he also took pride in the way he kept his home.

In Richard's dining area he had a maple wood table, six matching chairs and a china cabinet. The china cabinet had two glass shelves one on each side and a cabinet with doors that opened in the middle. That's where Richard kept his safe deposit box.

The TV in the living room was at least 42 inches and it looked real big. Back then we didn't have flat screens, we had big boxes and a 42 inch was considered one of the biggest. Richard's whole apartment was neat and comfortable.

Richard took me to the living room so I could sit down. The furniture was tan, comfortable and expensive. "Have a seat Ang, let me cut on the TV for you. What you wanna watch?"

We watched TV for a little while in the living room. We talked, laughed, kissed and touched. One touch led to another, and we eventually found ourselves inside of the bedroom.

Richard's bed faced the door and the 32 inch television sat on a TV stand against the wall to the right. The bed was the first thing I noticed when I walked in his room. It was a king size, dressed in all white, the comforter, the sheets and the bed shams. The headboard was made like a bookshelf, with nightstands connected and built-in lights.

We continued to kiss, touch and foreplay. We undressed each other and took a shower together. After we got out of the shower, we continued our foreplay and Richard and I had sex for the first time.

The next morning Richard woke up with so much energy. He was jumping up and down on the bed naked, acting silly. He made me French Toast, turkey bacon, and he served it to me while I was still in bed. When we were getting ready to leave, Richard started acting silly again and threw some cold water on me while I was taking a shower. He came in the bathroom, slid the shower door open and threw the cold water on me. I screamed "Richard Stop!" He laughed at me. Richard got in the shower with me, we both washed up, got dressed, and left. When we got in the car, Richard gave me a kiss on my lips, looked me in my eyes and said, "I love you."

I hated leaving. When it was time to leave Richard I always got sad. I was especially sad on this day because it was my first time spending the night with Richard. It was the first time I had sex with him. I felt so attached. Another reason why I was sad was because I was going to be in trouble for spending the night out. I was only seventeen. Helen let me go out on dates with Richard and she let me go out with other guys, but I couldn't spend the night out. So I knew when I got home Helen was going to give me the talk, about staying out, and not calling. I knew I would not be able to go out for a day or two. I never remember being really punished while I was living with Helen even if I stayed out all night.

It seemed like every time Richard was taking me home, the song Secret Lovers by Pebbles and BabyFace would come on the radio in the car, making my ride home even sadder.

Right before school started September 1986, Richard took me and his little brother Donnell school shopping. Richard picked me up from 142nd Street and then we went to 132nd street to get Donnell. Donnell was with Velma, Richard's mother. When we pulled up, Velma was standing on the stoop with Donnell. Velma walked over to the car, said "Hello," and left. Donnell got in the car, and we drove off to go school shopping at the mall in New Jersey.

We went straight to the highway and across the bridge to New Jersey. It was still early, and none of us had had breakfast yet so we stopped at IHOP. Richard always talked about Donnell, and I had seen him outside riding his bike when I was with Richard. But I had never spent any time with Donnell.

As soon as we sat down at the table in IHOP, Richard began to act silly. The waitress sat us in a booth. I sat on one side of the table and Richard and Donnell next to each other on the other side. "Yo, you think she pretty?" Richard asked Donnell. Donnell didn't say anything. He looked at Richard, as if he wanted to say, come on now, why are you putting me on the spot. "Go ahead, you can say it, she's pretty right?" Donnell nodded his head, yes. During breakfast, we laughed and talked about life and what was expected for the school year. Richard liked to joke with Donnell, but he also was very serious with Donnell when it came to school.

Richard made sure he got everything Donnell needed, including his book bag and school supplies. He made sure I had everything too.

Once we were done shopping, we stopped to get something to eat. Donnell wanted McDonalds. So, we stopped at McDonald's and we all got something to eat before going back to the city.

I loved Donnell, he was a good kid. He was kind, polite and he had a loving spirit. Donnell didn't talk a lot when we went shopping but I could tell he really looked up to Richard. What ever Richard told Donnell to do, he would do it. If we were out and Richard saw Donnell some place he wasn't supposed to be, he would tell Donnell to go home and Donnell would go home. If Donnell did not behave himself in school or out of school, Richard would put Donnell on punishment. One day in the summer of 1986 I was in the car with Richard and we saw Donnell on the hill. He had his gold chain on that Richard bought him for his birthday. Richard pulled over; Donnell was sitting on his bike. Richard said, "Yo, come here." Donnell walked over to the car. "Didn't I tell you not to wear that chain when you are hanging out in the street?" "Yeah," Donnell answered. "So why you got it on?" Richard was really upset with Donnell. "Take it off and give it to me now. You can't just be wearing this chain all over. Niggas are hungry and they will kill you for that chain." Donnell took the chain off and passed it to Richard. "I'm going to take it with me. The next time you wanna wear it ask me and if I feel like it's safe and appropriate, I will let you wear it. "

Richard said, "I'm going to call you tomorrow Donnell. Make sure you get all of your stuff. You need some help?" Donnell said, "Nah I got it." I said bye to Donnell, and he said bye to me. As Donnell walked aways from the car, Richard said, "Yo, I love you and don't be outside too late." Donnell said ok and Richard pulled off. After Richard dropped Donnell off, he dropped me off on 142nd Street.

Richard never formally introduced me to his mother until after she got clean, but he did introduce me to his father, Shelton. Richard did not have the same last name as his father, Porter came from his mother's side of the family. Shelton's last name was Scott.

The first time I met Shelton he was standing by Lenox Terrace. Lenox

Terrace is a large apartment complex in Harlem and the buildings are located between Lenox and Fifth Avenue from 132nd to 135th street. Shelton was standing right in front of a Bar Lounge named CandleLight. We were in the car driving by when Richard saw his father. "I want you to meet my father." He made a u-turn and then another u-turn. Richard pulled up and Shelton noticed him right away. Richard said, "Come on let's go say hi." I got out of the car and we both walked towards Shelton, and he walked towards us. Richard immediately said to Shelton, "I want you to meet my new girlfriend, Angela. She is a good girl." Richard always included that I was a good girl, whenever he introduced me to anyone. Shelton smiled and said, "Nice to meet you." Richard and I had not been together that long before he introduced me to his father so I was not expecting him to introduce me as his girlfriend, but he did.

Shelton was a nice-looking man. Richard looked a lot like his father only thing Shelton's skin color was a few tones lighter. Shelton and Richard had the same box head, big jaws, and a very similar face. Shelton was really friendly and he always greeted me politely after meeting me. I was quiet so I didn't say much but Shelton was always upbeat, pleasant and he had a good spirit.

Richard and his father seemed to have a good relationship. Richard never drove by Lenox Terrace without checking to see if his father was outside.

Richard's mother and father were not together when I met Richard's father. Richard's father was in a relationship with another woman at the time. I don't remember her name but I met her a few times. I'm not sure if they were married but I know Shelton had a little daughter with her. Her name was Nelly. Richard had another sister from his father named Misa and then he had Pat his sister with whom he shared the same mother and father. I hadn't met Pat yet. Richard talked about her once in awhile, but I had never seen, met or spoken to her before.

Richard came to see me every night before he went home. Some nights he would take me out to eat before he went in and some nights he would just give me a kiss and say good night.

One of my most rememberable nights is when Richard took me for a ride on his motorcycle. I was so scared, but it was a lot of fun.

Richard came riding down 142nd Street on his motorcycle. Alpo was with him and on a motorcycle as well. Once again, it was like a movie scene as everyone watched like they were in a dream. To see Richard and Alpo together was not uncommon at that time but, to some, it was like a special treat.

When I first met Richard, I never remember him being around a lot of people. I remember him being with his friend T-Money, his cousin Red and this guy named Maurice. Alpo seemed to be the only person he actually hung out with on a personal level.

When they rode up I was standing in front of my building on the stoop. Richard pulled up and shone the light on me. "What's up?" he asked me. I smiled and asked if he was talking to me. I walked over to Richard, he was sitting on his motorcycle, " Get on the back." I jumped on the back of the motorcycle.

"Hold my waist." I wrapped my arm around his waist. "No don't wrap your arms around me just hold my waist. Don't be scared." I said, "I'm not scared this is my first time riding on a motorcycle. "

Richard and Alpo geared up their motorcycles. They both drove to the light and stood at the red light parallel to one another. I sat behind Richard, holding his waist tight. The light turned green, and they pulled off and drove straight down142nd Street to FDR Drive. Richard and Alpo both merged onto F.D.R. Drive. It was late, so F.D.R. Drive was pretty empty. As soon as they got on the highway, they both sped up. I really believe they were racing. The wind was hitting my face and taking my breath away. I put my head on Richard's right shoulder and looked ahead until the speeding was over. We got off on 96th Street and went to One Fish Two Fish, a restaurant that was on Madison Avenue. We got something to eat and Richard took me home. We took the streets back to 142nd Street. I was happy because the streets felt safe compared to riding on the highway. The F.D.R. Drive is narrow and curvy. I never liked riding on F.D.R. Drive in a car, it always seemed dangerous, and riding a motorcycle on the F.D.R. Drive seemed even more dangerous. Riding on the street just felt more safe. The streets were brighter with street lights. The traffic lights stopped Richard from riding so fast. Honestly, I was happy when I got back home and off of his motorcycle. That may have been the last time I rode on Richard's motorcycle.

Richard was busy during the week, and we didn't really get a chance to spend time with each other, so he dedicated Sundays to me. Every Sunday we spent together we went out to eat, to the movies, shopping and sometimes we just went to his place in Harmon Cove to hang out.

I liked going to Richard's place on Sundays. Richard loved to cook for me. One of his favorites things to make was steak. Richard loved a ribeye steak. I remember the first time he made me a steak like it was yesterday. It was one of our Sundays together and Richard decided that he wanted us to chill at his place in Harmon Cove. "I make the best steak, Ang. Wait until you taste it, nobody's steak is better than me."

While he was making the steak Richard would call me in the kitchen," Ang look at this, this is how you make a steak. You season it, you put some butter on it and then you put it underneath the broiler." Richard led me through every step of making the steak, it was more like we made the steak together. After the steak was done, I have to say the steak was good. And every time Richard cooked for me it was good.

That summer of 1986 was the summer Richard and I really bonded.

.

HERE COMES THE HATE...

When you are dealing with a man of great caliber like Richard Porter you can expect hate, jealousy, envy, and issues with other women. It's all part of the game.

Sometimes the hate comes disguised as care and the hater doesn't even know they're hating.

I found out about Maria in the summer of 1986. Maria was Richard's other girlfriend from 140th Street. Maria and Richard had history together that I knew nothing about until after I started dating Richard.

When I moved back to Harlem, others in Harlem knew that Richard was dating Maria but I didn't know. I didn't know who Richard was and I sure didn't know who his girlfriend was. I was just moving back to Harlem and was out of the loop. I didn't know who the big-time drug dealers was and I didn't care. I didn't know who the fly girls were and I didn't care. I didn't know a lot of people and a lot of people didn't know me.

Helen called me into her room one day in the summertime to ask me about Richard and Maria. Honestly, I'm not sure if I knew about Maria or not at this time. I know one thing, it didn't matter. Yvette and Netta were already in the room with Helen. "Did you know Richard has a girlfriend?" I stayed quiet. "He has a girlfriend named Maria." I forget what was said after that but I do remember Helen asking Yvette and Netta, "Who looks better, Angie or Marie?" Netta and Yvette both answered and said that Maria looked better. I was like oh shit, right in the face.

I had been dating Richard for a couple of months already. We went out on dates all the time, he gave me money, and brought me nice gifts. When I met Richard I was with Yvette and Maria was not an issue then, so why was she an issue now? Why should I get involved? As a matter of fact I don't remember Yvette saying anything about Maria at the beginning, when Richard and I first met.

I forget how the conversation ended that day with all of us, but I do remember the conversation I had with Richard about Maria.

It was a Saturday early afternoon. I was at Ina and Debbie's beauty parlor on 146th Street between Bradhurst and 8th Avenue. Richard came to pick me up. A lot of females got their hair done at Ina and Debbie's salon. They knew all the gossip of the street life of Harlem during that time.

I didn't know Richard was coming to pick me up, but I was happy. Even more exciting was the fact that I forgot where his car was so he was walking. Richard and I walked together holding hands back to 142nd Street. That meant a lot to me and I know Richard meant for it to mean a lot to me. He was making a statement not to just me but to everyone we walked by and everyone they told.

We walked up 145th Sstreet, from 8th Avenue to 7th Avenue, then we turned on 7th Ave and continued to 142nd Street. As we walked past 144th Street there were a few guys standing out in front of Sickle's spot. I can't remember if any of the guys said hi to Richard or not but I do recall getting an energy as if they did not like him. Richard and I walked straight to 142nd for the most part, he said "What's up?" to a few people but we kept it moving, walking, holding hands, and talking.

We talked about the conversation I had with Helen, Yvette and Netta. "So what happened? What did Helen say?"

"She asked me did I know about Maria. I didn't say anything, I just stayed quiet."

"They are jealous of you Ang, why is Yvette saying something about Maria now."

"I don't know but this is becoming too much. I don't think we should see each other anymore."

When we reached 142nd and Lenox Avenue, we crossed the street and sat on the stoop at Minisink Townhouse on 142nd in Lenox Avenue.

While we were sitting down talking, one of the guys from 144th Street and 7th Avenue came riding down the block. The guy had seen us walk by 144th earlier and now he was riding down 142nd slowing down, eyeing me in front of Richard.

I paid him no attention at all. I realized then that Richard was not liked or respected by some.

We continued talking. Richard was honest and told me that he and Maria had been dating since they were 13 years old. Richard's exact words were, "Ang she don't do anything wrong, I can't just leave her." I guess he was saying she didn't do anything wrong to him like cheat with other guys.

Richard started to tear up because I told him we should not date anymore. Daniel, Richard's cousin, pulled up, got out of the car and walked over to where we were sitting. As soon as Daniel approached, Richard said, "Yo Daniel, she is cutting me off. She cutting off the King."

Richard said, "I love her but I'm in love with you." I loved Richard's honesty and I understood what he was saying. His conscience would not let him abandon his relationship with Maria just because he'd found someone else he loved. I decided I was going to still date Richard.

Helen and her daughters didn't like that I continued to see Richard. They felt like our relationship would bring problems to our household.

Yvette particularly hated that I still saw Richard. She would shout at me anything true or false she heard about Richard, hoping to hurt my feelings. One time Richard and I were standing downstairs talking in front of my building on 142nd Street. Yvette came downstairs. She looked at Richard, Richard said, "Why you looking at me like that?" "Oh Richard please, you mess with my sister," Yvette responded.

Richard said, "And your sister is a hoe." Yvette got upset.

I don't think Yvette said anything else after Richard said what he said about her sister.

Richard and I walked off and got in his car. When we got in the car we talked about what had just happened. "Ang she was trying to hurt your feelings. That's why I said what I said. I went to see her sister but it's nothing, she was trying to play you." The fact that Richard said what he said, I was sure that her sister was not a concern.

Maria on the other hand was not happy about me. I'm not saying I was happy with knowing about her but whatever Richard had with her didn't stop me from feeling secure with what Richard and I had. Their relationship did not bother me.

Maria always started trouble with me. If it wasn't her starting trouble, then it was her family or friends. If I was walking down the block and if one of her friends saw me they would purposefully bump my shoulder as we walked by each other or they would call me a name like "you yellow bitch." Maria and her friends would call the house phone and say things like, "That's why you are adopted" or they would call me a "bum bitch," and they would say stupid shit like, "That's why you shop on Third Avenue." Maria and her family had a very distinct voice. It wasn't hard to tell when it was them prank calling, they were troublemakers.

One time Netta and I were walking down Maria's block and Maria called me again a "bum bitch." My foster sister said, "Oh no! You are going to say something back to her right now." We walked up to Maria. I was scared to death because I heard that Maria could fight. I said,"What you wanna do?" Maria stepped back and said, "Oh please, look at you with your fifty-dollar sneakers compared to my two hundred dollar Gucci boots. Look at your little name chain compared to my two-thousand dollar chain." I didn't care about what Maria was saying because I liked my name chain, I liked wearing sneakers. I had plenty of clothes and shoes that Richard bought for me. I always chose to wear sneakers and jeans unless the occasion called for different. I was saying to myself who does that when they are about to fight. I put my hands up and threw the first punch and my left fist landed right in her face. She stepped back again and said, "Oh no, you hit me in the face." That's when I was like oh my God this chick is about to fuck me up. Somebody said, "Fuck her up Maria!" and that's when we started to fight. The people in the block broke the fight up and then Netta and I went home.

A few months after I had a fight with Maria my foster sister Yvette also got into a fight with Maria at Daniel's mother's apartment which was Richard's aunt, Joanne. Maria used to hang out at Joanne's apartment all the time. I'm not sure what happened but that fight between my foster sister Yvette and Maria really made my foster mother not like Richard.

My foster mother told me I could not go out with Richard anymore.

I beeped Richard and he called me back.

"Helen told me I can't see you anymore."

"Why?"

"Because of Maria. She said Maria is your girlfriend and as long as you date Maria she was not going to allow me to see you. " "Tell Helen I wanna talk to her, ask her if I can come up there right now and talk to her?"

I said, "Hold on." I was in the kitchen; I laid the phone handle down on the kitchen cabinet and went to ask Helen. She was lying on her bed watching TV. "Helen, Richard said can he come and talk to you?" "Yeah he can come talk to me," Helen answered. "When do he wanna talk to me?" "He said, right now." Helen said, "Okay tell him to come."

I went back to the phone and told Richard.

While Richard was upstairs we received a prank call. Helen told Richard to answer the phone. He answered the phone and recognized the voice. He called whoever was on the phone a "stupid bitch" and told them to stop calling. Richard said he knew the voice and it was Maria and her friends.

Richard told Helen that he loved me. Helen told him that Maria was causing too much trouble. Helen still said I could not see Richard but I continued to see him anyway. I thought it was unfair that I could not see Richard anymore but Yvette could continue to see Daniel. Richard treated me much better than how Daniel treated Yvette. Yvette always got into fights with females because of Daniel.

I'm not saying that Richard was perfect. I'm not saying that Richard never hurt my feelings because he did. I'd seen Richard with another female who was not Maria, it was Heidi. Heidi and I went to the same high school. She knew of me, and I knew of her. Heidi was light skinned, with "nice hair," and she had a nice shape. Heidi was a pretty girl. Anyway I was on 145th and Lenox when I saw Heidi and her friends in the car with Richard. Richard was driving his Jeep Wrangler. It was a beautiful day and the top was off so it was impossible for me not to see what was going on. I was right on the corner of 145th Street and Lenox Avenue, in front of the Kennedy Fried Chicken spot. I was getting a banana strawberry ice cream shake. I always loved the shakes from Kennedy because they were made with Breyers ice cream.

Richard came driving down 145th Street and made a quick left turn going towards Esplanade Gardens. Before he made the turn, he noticed me, and he noticed that I noticed him. His Jeep was filled with Heidi and her friends. Heidi and I had mutual friends and some of the females that were in the Jeep was supposed to be my friends also.

I walked back to my block, 142nd Street and Lenox Avenue. Ten minutes later Richard drove up. He came to explain. "Ang I was dropping Heidi off for her father, her father asked me yp drop her off." Richard told me he was doing some business with her father, something to do with music. I can't really remember. As long as Richard respected me and showed me he cared about my feelings I was quick to let the little shit go. The quicker he addressed it, the quicker I let it go. Actually when I saw Heidi and her friends in the car with Richard, I was more hurt about the other females being in the Jeep with her. I thought they were my friends. I was sure that they knew that I was dating Richard, but I could be wrong, maybe they didn't.

After I saw Heidi in the car with Richard I didn't like her. We went to the same high school, so we rode the bus together and we had a few staring matches on the bus. Our eyes would be connected, eye to eye, until one of us broke and said something. If it was Heidi she usually said something like, " Is it a problem?" And, when it was me I usually asked, " What the fuck are you looking at?"

One day I was walking past 144th Street and 7th Avenue. Heidi was standing outside. As I walked by, she was staring at me. I said, " You yellow bitch." There were a few guys standing around. This was Heidi's turf and the guys didn't like that I called her a yellow bitch. I recall hearing a guy say something like "get outta here with the shit." Anyway, I kept walking.

Heidi and I ran into each other another time. We were in front of Drew Hamilton projects. She asked me if she could talk to me. I said yes. The conversation was weird and it always made me think weirdly of Heidi afterwards. "We are both Pisces," I said. "I don't give a fuck about us both being Pisces. Stop staring in my fucking face". I walked off and that was the end of that conversation. Heidi had a staring problem, that's what she said, in my opinion she was starting trouble.

I only seen Richard with Heidi one time and I let it go but I'm sure he was still fucking her. One day when we were at his apartment in

Harmon Cove there was some hair in the bathroom sink and it was the same color as Heidi's hair. Heidi's hair color was different from Maria's and mine. There weren't to many girls in Harlem with that hair color and I knew Richard was not fucking a blonde white chick.

I found the hair in the bathroom sink in the hallway. I was probably making a shit and didn't want Richard to know. I used the hallway bathroom instead of the bathroom in the bedroom. I picked the hair up with my fingers and held it up in front of me. I walked into Richard's bedroom. "Whose hair is this?" Richard didn't say anything, he just had this like what are you talking about look. Richard always gave the crazy face with a smirk when he was wrong. I forget what happened after that, I can't remember what he told me. I can't remember if it was a lie or the truth.

Not too long after that incident I heard Heidi was pregnant. No, I don't remember how I heard about Heidi being pregnant or who told me. But I do remember the conversation Richard and I had about Heidi being pregnant. We were together one day and I didn't ask him about Heidi being pregnant right away but when he asked me to have his baby, that's when I said something.

I screamed at him "Let Heidi have your baby and stop asking me to have your baby." Richard was surprised that I knew. Richard said, "I don't want her to have my baby, she's fucking Alpo." I said, "You fucking her. Let her have your baby." Richard said, "She ain't even pregnant no more, she wanted to keep it but I told her father and he made her have an abortion." That was all I needed to hear. And the fact that Heidi was fucking Alpo, let me know she was nothing to be worried about, when it came to Richard and my relationship.

I'm sure Richard was fucking a lot of females in Harlem. As a matter of fact, I heard someone say, "Rich always on top of a bitch". It didn't affect me because I knew Maria and Heidi were a wrap, even if Richard did like Heidi it was not enough for him to swallow his pride and accept the fact that she was fucking or fucked Alpo. I really believe if Heidi didn't fuck Alpo she might have had a chance with gaining Richard's extended love.

Yvette used to always say Richard is sneaky. Because when he did his shit, it was hard to get evidence. The females that he was fucking were not trying to let me know. They wouldn't dare fuck up their relationship with Richard. And Richard always did his shit tastefully and he never put me in a disrespectful situation. Daniel was always disrespecting Yvette, not only was he disrespectful but one time he gave Yvette a black eye and Helen didn't do anything. She called Daniel into her room and she told him "Don't put your hands on my fucking daughter." Helen didn't make Yvette stop seeing Daniel. We used to call Yvette "Sister" from the movie Sparkle because Sister's man was always whopping her ass and Yvette was always coming home with a bruise. Netta is the who called her Sister first. Netta said I was Sparkle and and she was the other sister. We used make jokes about Daniel hitting Yvette but it really was not funny. Daniel was not right one time; he had a girl in the car right on our block on 142nd Street. I don't know what he was trying to prove but Yvette saw Daniel, ran to his car and tried to open up the car door but Daniel drove off. Now that was disrespectful. Yvette got into fights with Daniel all the time. To her she was fighting him back, In my eyes he was beating her ass and she should never have had to fight him. Richard had never put his hands on me. Yvette also got into plenty of fights with females because of Daniel. It was not right that Helen was stopping me from seeing Richard

I never stopped seeing Richard. Now we had to sneak around in order to do anything together. And for this reason we never thought to take pictures because I didn't want any evidence.

We still spent time together on Sunday even if we had to sneak. One Sunday we were sitting in his car on Lenox Avenue, between 141st Street and 142nd Street. We couldn't sit in 142nd Street anymore because it was just too hot. And all Helen's and Yvette's flunkies would run and tell Helen if they saw me with Richard. We were sitting in the car talking.

Richard said, " Yo your sister is crazy, look this letter she wrote to Dan."

Richard gave me the letter to read. I don't remember everything that was in the letter but I do know my foster sister Yvette was pointing out to Daniel how Richard takes me out on Sundays and how Richard brought me a name chain. Richard said, "Dan said come on Rich you causing problems doing all this stuff with Angie."

Richard said, "Ang, they are jealous of you, and stop being so nice, when Yvette says things to hurt your feelings say something back to hurt her feelings." I said, "I can't hurt people's feelings. I don't like to hurt other people." "Well they don't care about hurting you, Ang, people are not nice, stop being so nice to everyone. They don't care about you."

Richard always tried to school me on how jealous, envious and selfish people were, but I really didn't get it, I had to learn on my own.

SECRET LOVERS

We never stopped seeing each other. Once Helen told us to stop seeing each other, we just started sneaking around and being secret lovers. Most of the time I had to cut school to be with Richard. Those were the only hours I could get away without anyone looking for me. Richard didn't like that I cut school but I loved it. For me, It was more like bringing your child to work day. I was able to see what Richard's day to day life was like. It was fun. We went shopping, took care of his business and chilled at Richard's apartment.

Richard always picked me up from downtown when I cut school, somewhere near my school. No matter where I met Richard, I always went to school first. It was important for me to go to home room so I could be marked present in school. Most of the time when we met, it was after 2nd or 3rd period.

We always planned the night before so I knew where to meet Richard, and what time to be there. Things were different back then, your word was your bond. There were no cell phones so there wasn't no changing plans at the last minute. You had to stick to the plan.

Sometimes we met at a street location and sometimes we met at a store location.

There was a men's boutique store not far from Julia Richmond that Richard use to shop at. I can't remember the name of the store but the store was located on 2nd Avenue between 65th and 66th Street. Richard told me to meet him at the boutique one day after I cut school. It was my first-time meeting Richard at this men's Boutique. I'm not sure what time we met but I'm sure it was in the morning. When I got to the boutique Richard was outside waiting for me. We went inside the store.

As soon as Richard walked through the door he was treated as royalty.

"What's up Rich?"

"What you got for me? What's new?"

"We just go some new silk tee shirts in I think you will like."

"Let me see them." The guy brought Richard the tee shirt. Richard opened it up, "What size is this?""That's a large, if you wanna try a medium let me know.""Nah I'm gonna take the large. Do you have any other colors?""Yeah we have two other colors, let me show you." Richard said he liked all three. "How much are these shirts? Two hundred for one." I thought, oh my God two hundred dollars for one tee shirt.

"Let me get all three for five hundred." The sales guy said, "I can give you all three for five fifty." "Ok, let me get them,"

After Richard was finished, we went straight to Jersey so Richard could take care of his personal business, like paying his utility bills. When Richard was done taking care of his personal business, we went to his house to chill.

I remember one time Richard picked me up on 68th Street and 3rd Ave. I left school early in the morning and met Richard. Richard had to take care of his business business. We rode uptown and stopped to get breakfast from Texas Grill. Texas Grill was a restaurant located around 148th Street on St. Nicholas Avenue. Richard loved their grilled cheese sandwiches and that was one of Richard's favorites breakfast spots. A lot of guys that Richard knew used to go to Texas Grill in the morning. Now that I think about it, they were probably taking care of business with Richard. Because when we were sitting outside in the car not too far from Texas Grill eating there was guys that drove up and went inside Texas Grill. Then Richard's beeper would go off, next thing I know Richard says, "I'll be right back". So yeah I didn't process it back then but I'm sure that's what was going on when I think about it today.

After we finished eating, Richard handled his business and made his rounds. One day Richard pulled up in front of a tenement on 148th Street. His cousin Red was standing on the stoop. Richard got out of the car, and I stayed in the car watching. I always watched Richard when he got out of the car. Richard walked up to the building, put one foot on the step and started talking to his cousin Red. While Richard was talking to Red, a pregnant female walked up, she was a crack head, I could tell. Richard looked at the pregnant female and said, "What you want, get out of here, they bet not sell nothing to you, you're pregnant." The female didn't say anything, she looked ashamed and walked off. "Don't sell her anything, I don't want y'all selling to pregnant women." Richard got back in the car, and we drove off.

Richard went from block-to-block and spot-to-spot, He picked up shoe boxes full of money. He still had his apartment in Fort Lee so we would go there to count the money. I helped Richard keep track of each account. I would let him know if a stack was short with a red highlight and the difference written down next to the name on the balance line. The accounts were named as blocks, areas, and code names. Government names were never used.

Even though we were not supposed to see each other, everyone in the house knew that we were still seeing each other. Living in Helen's house had become very uncomfortable for me because Yvette and Netta were constantly giving me attitude.

Sometimes I would pretend to be interested in other guys just to try to take the attention off of Richard and me. But that didn't work.

I remember once when I was home, I was talking to this guy that liked me. I forget his name but I believe he was an ex-police officer. Anyway we were standing in the hallway next to the bathroom. Yvette walked by us and said, "She is strung out on Richard, I know somebody that looks better than her that I can hook you up with." I was like ok. In my mind I was saying we'll hook him up so he can leave me the hell alone.

Richard and I snuck around for a while until Richard got tired of the sneaking around and decided to get me my own apartment.

The day that we went looking at apartments I was so happy. Richard told me to leave school early. I left school early and met him some where around my school. As soon as I got in the car, we went straight to Jersey. Richard pulled up in front of his realtor's office on Palisades Avenue not too far away from a McDonald's. "Wait right here. I will be right back." Richard came back outside with a guy that was his realtor. The guy got in his car and Richard got in his car. "We are going to follow him, he's going to take us to see a few apartments". I said ok. The realtor took us to see a few apartments but the only apartment I remember is the apartment I picked to live in. The apartment I picked was in Cliffside Park on George Rd. The building was condominium and the apartment was small and the outside was dark brown brick with brown panels around the top. I liked it, the apartment was a one bedroom with two full bathrooms. One bathroom was in the hallway and the other bathroom was in the master bathroom. The unit had a patio right off the living with a glass sliding door. I liked the apartment and so did Richard. He really liked the fact that building had a parking garage. Richard and I decided that we were going to take the apartment.

It was the winter of 1987 right before my eighteenth birthday when Richard got me my apartment, our apartment. The plan was for me to move once I turned eighteen. Once I turned eighteen I could leave Helen's house and the foster care system without getting in any trouble or anyone making me go back to a foster home.

I didn't move into my apartment right away because I was not eighteen yet and honestly I did not move into my apartment once I turned eighteen, because I felt guilty about leaving Helen's home. I felt like I was doing something wrong and I was scared about what they would think about me.

Even though I waited to move into my own apartment, we still went shopping for furniture, home appliances, home supplies and home goods.

Richard loved shopping, not just for clothes, cars, and jewelry. Richard loved shopping for pots and pans, sheets, towels, and silverware. We would always laugh and talk about how all those things were so scarce when we were growing up. We laughed about having only one sheet with little beads all over it or not having a washcloth to wash up with. We laughed about the days we had to wait until there was a spoon and bowl available so we could eat our cereal.

Our day of shopping for my apartment felt like husband and wife. We went to Hoffman Koos when I skipped school. Richard loved

Hoffman Koos. My living room and bedroom set came from Hoffman Koos and I loved it. Hoffman Koos was a popular furniture store back in the 80's. My living room was off white Italian leather. The coffee table and the end tables were made of glass. My bedroom was off white Italian lacquer with gold trimming. My bed faced my dresser with the mirror. The mirror was trimmed with gold and the dresser drawer knobs were all gold. My headboard was trimmed with gold. I loved my apartment.

We did a lot of things when were sneaking around. We went shopping, out to eat, took care of business including having sex all of the time. Eventually after having almost a year of unprotected sex, I got pregnant.

I had a feeling I was pregnant; I knew right away. I was tired all the time and I was eating more. My body felt drained. When I got pregnant it was May 1987, it was warm outside. I woke up one night around 1 am and I was starving. I got dressed and went to Kennedy Fried Chicken on 145th Street and Lenox Avenue. I was craving a cheeseburger from Kennedy. I used to love their cheeseburgers but I could never eat a whole cheeseburger, well not this night, I went to Kennedy got me a cheeseburger and ate every bit of that cheeseburger. I knew something was not right after I ate a whole cheeseburger from Kennedy.

Helen noticed I was sleeping and eating more so she made me an appointment with Dr Calloway. Dr. Calloway was an African American GYN doctor. His office was located in Lenox Terrace. Doctor Calloway was the neighborhood GYN, and a lot of women in Harlem went to him. Well, he was the doctor that the women in my foster family used.

I beeped Richard, he called me back." I think I'm pregnant Richard." "You probably are pregnant." I could hear the excitement in Richard's voice. "I've been sleeping a lot too, they say that fathers get pregnancy symptoms too." I laughed. "Well Helen noticed and she is making me go to the doctor. My appointment is today. I will beep you when I'm done."

I went to Doctor Calloway, I believe my foster sister Netta came with me. I'm not 100 percent sure. But I remember Helen knowing my results before me. As soon as I got home Helen called me on the phone. She said, "I knew you was pregnant." Back then there was no such thing as confidentiality, especially when it came to black doctors and black mothers. Especially GYN doctors.

Helen said, "Beep Richard and tell him I want to see him." I said ok and hung up the phone. As soon as I hung up, I beeped Richard. I couldn't wait to tell Richard that I was pregnant. I didn't even process the fact that Helen knew my pregnancy results before I knew. It didn't matter at that time because I was happy. Richard had been asking me to have a baby for so long. I would finally be able to give Richard something that he could not give to himself. And something that he wanted.

Richard called me back. As soon as he said hello, I said, "I'm pregnant." Richard said, "I knew you was pregnant." "Yeah, well, Helen told me to tell you she wants to see you." Richard said, "What she wanna see me for?"

"I guess she wants to talk to you about me being pregnant." "Where is she?" "She's at the number spot on 136th Street." "Okay I'm coming to get you and we going around there together."

When I got in the car, Richard was so happy. I had finally gotten pregnant. He kept saying he wanted me to have his baby and he had been trying to get me pregnant for a whole year. Richard thought it was strange that I had not gotten pregnant yet. One time he said, " I think you got an abortion and didn't tell me." I told him I never got an abortion. I also assume he was playing when he asked me if I had an abortion.

When we got around 136th Street, Richard parked the car. There was a parking space on the same block not too far from the number spot. I went to the door to let Helen know we were outside. Helen came outside. Richard and I were standing in front of the number spot together.

Helen said, "You know Angie is pregnant right?"

Richard stood back on his legs and he said, "Yeah, I know she's pregnant."

Helen said, "So what are you going to do?"

Richard said, "What do you mean, what am I going to do? I'm going to take care of her and my baby. It ain't nothing but a thing."

Helen looked at me. "Angie, you wanna have this baby?" "Yes." Helen said, "Okay" and went back into the number spot.

We walked back to the car and drove off.

A few days later I decided to permanently move into my apartment in Cliffside, New Jersey. I finally got the courage to leave Helen's apartment and go stay in my own apartment in New Jersey. I did not tell Helen or her daughters I was leaving. I just moved to my apartment and they found out later that I had my own apartment. I'm not sure how they found out but I'm sure Richard's cousin Daniel told Yvette because that was her man. And it really was no secret because I was 18 and pregnant so they knew Richard and I were definitely still seeing each other.

WINDY TIME

I moved into my apartment in the beginning of the summer in 1987. I didn't have a car or a driver's license. I didn't have to worry about getting back and forth to school at the time because it was the summertime.

Richard still had his apartment in Harmon Cove but he stayed with me at least three nights of the week and we never went a day without seeing each other.

Richard always made sure I was ok. He always made sure I had money, food, and he made sure my bills were paid.

Richard kept stacks of money at my apartment. He kept it in my dresser drawer, the top left drawer. Every night Richard came home he would empty his pockets, take his jewelry off piece by piece and neatly place them on the top of the dresser. I can still picture Richard taking off his shirt, pulling it over his head and flexing with his tee shirt on, walking back and forth talking with his boxers on.

Richard was a morning man, he took care of business so he was up pretty early. I used to watch Richard get dressed in the morning. Richard would stand in front of my bed and get dressed. Then he would sit on the foot of the bed and count his money. One day Richard put a stack of money on the top of the dresser and said, " Ang this is for you. Whatever I put on the dresser is for you and whatever I put in the drawer is for me." Richard never left our home without leaving me money. He wanted to make sure I had money for safety and pleasurable reasons.

Every morning I would sit up in my bed, comb my hair, look in the mirror and watch him get dressed at the same time. One morning Richard saw me watching him and he said, "You need to get up, go to the mall or something instead of combing your hair and looking in the mirror all day." I couldn't say anything because he was right. All I did was sit in bed all day. When I was pregnant it took a lot of energy out of me. I was sick a lot, so I did stay home.

Later on that day I took Richard's advice and I went to the mall. I called a cab to take me to Garden State Mall in a New Jersey. I was at the mall for a little while before I started getting lightheaded, dizzy, and nauseous. I found a seat next to an entrance, called a cab and I went right back home.

I stayed home a lot so Richard always made sure the refrigerator and kitchen cabinet stayed filled up. I used to love cooking for Richard. Well, I used to love trying to cook for Richard. One time I made Mac and cheese. Richard was like, "What is this supposed to be?" I was so embarrassed.

We always went grocery shopping at night. Richard liked going to the grocery store when it was not crowded, if you ask me why, I would say because he loved clowning in the grocery store. Richard used to race down the aisles pushing the shopping cart, playing hide and go seek. He was playing with me, but I was not playing with him, but he didn't care. I would be looking for Richard all over the store. Once in a while Richard would go to the store without me especially if he needed to pick just a few things like cereal and milk. Richard always made sure we kept a lot of milk and his favorite cereal Sugar Smacks. I used to drink a gallon of milk a day and Richard thought it was crazy that I drank so much milk. One time Richard stopped by my apartment to drop off some groceries. Azie and Alpo were with Richard, and they came inside. I came out of my bedroom, and I said hello. Azie and Alpo both stood at the kitchen door while Richard put the groceries away. As he was putting the groceries away, he said to Azie and Alpo, "Yo, Ang drinks a gallon a milk a day, that's crazy right." Of course, I don't remember how Azie and Alpo responded but I know one thing, milk used to help my stomach. I used to vomit all the time. I didn't eat a lot and sometimes when I vomited, my stomach would jerk and it would cause pain. One time I vomited and blood was in the vomit. The doctor said it was because my stomach was empty. So whenever I felt like I needed to vomit I would drink milk first so the vomit could come out easy.

You could not tell me nothing then. I was grown, pregnant, and I had my family. I had my husband, a nice home, and our child was on the way. Just the way I dreamed it to be when I was younger. I was in LaLa fairy tale land for a little while, then It seemed like everything started to hit the fan.

A lot of shit started popping and it had an adverse effect on everything, including Richard's and my relationship.

It seemed like all the bull shit started right after Azie and five other people got shot up in the Bronx.

Buzz, buzz, buzz, that's all I kept hearing. It was Richard's beeper going off. Velma, Richard's mother, was beeping Richard back to back. It was August 22, 1987, a Saturday morning. Back then we took the weekends very serious as a self-care day. Velma started beeping Richard around 6:30am. It was 7am and Velma was still beeping, I couldn't take the beeping no more so I looked at Richard's beeper and noticed that it was his mother's number. "Richard your mother is beeping you like crazy. Something must be wrong, get up and call her back."

Richard called his mother. "Yeah, ma?" Then Richard got upset. "So what the fuck y'all calling me for? Why, you beeping me like you're crazy? What you want me to do!?" He hung up the phone, "I don't know why they're calling me, I don't have shit to do with that."

"What happened?" I asked.

"Azie got shot up last night, him and a few other people. I don't know why my mother is calling me. What do they want me to do?"

Later on that day, Richard got more information so he called to let me know what was going on.

I Immediately asked Richard what happened. " Azie was going to an apartment in the Bronx and they tried to rob him. " "Dam." "Yeah six people got shot and three of them are dead, they shot them executional style including a 13 year old little girl." "What's executional style? " The killers made them get down on their knees, cuffed their hands behind their backs and shot each of them." "Dam that's fucked up." "Azie, one of the dudes, and the 13 year old girl is in the hospital, in critical condition. But Charlie, Joanne and Myra did not survive." "Do they know who the killers are?" "I heard one of the guys was fucking with one of Azie sister's. This dude's name Kevin." "Wow." "Yeah this is why I told you that you can't have everybody over." Richard hung up the phone and we talked more about what happened when he got home.

It was not hard for the individuals responsible for this horrific crime to be caught because Azie was able to identify Kevin Clark.

On August 25, 1987 three days after the killings, Ronald Timmons from Jamaica Queens, who was 30 years old and Kevin Clark from the Bronx were arrested for murder and attempted murder.

On September 19 Henry Bolden, a third suspect, 28 years old, was picked up in Richmond, Virginia.

Before the situation happened with Azie, Richard stayed with me at my place in Cliffside Park all the time. After Azie got shot up, Richard began to really do things differently.

One time, we took a cab home to my place in New Jersey. Richard asked the cab driver to stop a few blocks from my apartment. "Yo stop right here, we are going to get out right here, how much I owe you." Richard paid the cab driver and we got out the cab and walked the rest of the way. It was dark outside. Jersey was different, there weren't many streetlights. Richard took my hand and we walked. I asked no questions—I just followed. I was always able to read Richard's energy, and this was no time for questions. I knew Richard was making sure he was not being followed, but what I did not know was why. I didn't know if Richard was worried about the police following him or if he was worried about someone trying to rob and harm us.

Richard never brought anyone else to my apartment after Azie and his crew got shot up. I started to get scared because of the way he was acting. Richard also told me not to bring anyone to my apartment, not even my friends. I had only brought two of my friends because Richard was picky and he felt like a few of my friends talked too much, so he told me they could never come.

I was scared to stay in my apartment by myself. I could not sleep. And, Richard moving the way he was, all paranoid and shit, made shit worse. I would stay up all night

sitting on my couch, watching the front door and the patio door. My couch was in the perfect position, I was able to keep my eyes on both entrances at the same time. Every day, that was my routine. I stayed up like a watch dog at night and slept restlessly through the day. This went on for the rest of the summer.

Every night I put the latch on the front door. I wanted to make sure no one could get in. I was worried that someone might get the keys from Richard and come to kill me. I was really scared.

Richard hated when he came home, and the latch was on the door. Sometimes, I would hear Richard drive into the garage. I could always tell when it was him. It was a certain way he pulled into the driveway, the speed of the car, the turn, and the smooth brake. I always knew when it was Richard. I listened as he drove into the garage and pulled into his parking spot. But sometimes I didn't hear him because I was asleep. That was rare though, because I was so scared that I was up most nights.

I remember, one night, Richard banged on the door and screamed my name. I thought I was dreaming. "Come on! Why is the latch on the door!? I need to be able to get in!" Shit, I guess we were both scared. I was scared of someone getting in and he was scared that someone might be following him. Shit was just scary and I did not want to stay there anymore if Richard did not stay with me.

Richard started staying with me less and less.

When we did stay together, we would stay at his place at Harmon Cove in Secaucus. Harmon Cove was a different type of vibe. And

I'm sure Richard felt more safe there since Harmon Cove had security guards. They knew who Richard was and Richard knew who they were. As soon as Richard walked through the door he would say "hello Sir" to the security guard. There were security cameras everywhere in the garage, in the building lobby, in the elevator, and cameras in the hallways on every floor. After Azie got shot up, every time Richard saw a security camera he would point to the security camera and say, "Look Ang that's a security camera." He always told me basketball players lived in Harmon Cove Towers so I guess he felt like if it was safe enough for the basketball players, it would be safe enough for him.

The whole idea of me moving into my own apartment was great. But I didn't think about how it would change the dynamic of our relationship. I don't believe Richard thought about it either. Before I moved into my own apartment it was like I never had enough time to spend with Richard. Now that I was available all the time, I realized how much time Richard didn't have to spend with me.

Azie getting shot up opened my eyes and mind up to concerns that I hadn't thought about. There was a lot of what ifs in my head. What If someone tries to kill me, what if someone tries to break into my apartment, what if someone follows Richard home, the list of what ifs in my head went on and on.

I was young and pregnant. Whenever Richard did not stay with me it made me upset. My emotions got the best of me. And, when Richard did not come to my apartment in Cliffside, I would threaten to throw his money and his jewelry down the toilet. I used to act like I was going to commit suicide and throw pills all over the floor. When Richard would finally come to my apartment, he really thought I was crazy. Everything would be all over the place because I'd had a tantrum. Yes, it was stupid, but I was young, pregnant, and paranoid.

I started running away from my apartment and Richard. I left my apartment in Jersey a few times to stay with different people in the city. I was running away to make Richard mad. I was also running away to stay somewhere I felt safe.

I never told Richard when I was leaving, I would just leave. I would not tell him where I was and I would not call him for days. He would get so mad at me.

I lost a lot of my shit staying with people. One time I ran away from Richard and I was staying downtown Manhattan with this lady I knew. I took a shower to cool off because it was a hot evening. I took my earrings, name chain, and name ring off and lay them down on the arm of the chair before I got in the shower. I was the only person in the apartment at the time. When I got out of the shower everything was still on the arm of the lazy boy chair. I put on something comfortable and sat down in the lazy boy chair and fell asleep.

When I woke up—all my jewelry was gone.

I asked her what happened to my jewelry, and she said she did not see any jewelry. I was like, "What the fuck?" She tried to ignore what was going on and asked me if I wanted something to eat. I was like, "Where the fuck is my jewelry?" I should have known better because I had a feeling she was a crackhead. I just never thought she would steal my shit. I was naive.

She could have asked me for money. Anyone who knew me would tell you that if I had it, you had it. I called Richard and he came to get me and took me home to my apartment in New Jersey. Richard was so upset that she stole my shit. He always said that I was too nice.

The summer of 1987 was over, and it was time for me to go back to school. I was staying at my apartment in New Jersey. Richard started staying with me a little more so I was not as scared. But the hassle of traveling back and forth to school was really taking a toll on me.

I traveled back and forth from New Jersey to New York using public transportation—and it was a lot. Every morning, I would take the bus to the Port Authority. Then I would have to walk through the tunnel, take the shuttle train to the East Side then take the 6 train to 68th Street and Lexington Avenue to get to Julia Richmond High School.

I could have taken a cab every morning and sometimes I did take a cab, but public transportation was faster on the week days in the morning. Now, on the weekends or in the evenings, I always took a cab to and from the city.

I had a rough pregnancy. I stayed sick. One day on the train, I got dizzy and I could not see anything. I asked quietly if someone could help me, and this white lady helped me off the train. She sat me down on the bench and sat next to me. She asked me if I was okay. I told her I was pregnant, and she immediately understood what was happening. The lady advised me to stay there for a while. I sat there until I was okay to continue to school. It started getting cold outside and the heavy coats made it even harder for me to travel. I wanted to stay home all the time, but I couldn't. Richard did not play when it came to school. If I did stay home, I would not answer the phone because I was afraid it might be Richard on the other end. If I stayed home Richard would lecture me like he was my parent.

The further I got into my pregnancy the less and less Richard and I were having sex. Richard said he didn't wanna have sex with me, he would always say, "Ang I don't wanna hit my baby's head." I used to say Richard "Please" and laugh. Richard was excited from the time I got pregnant. He was excited and curious. One time he put his fingers up my vagina and he said he could feel the baby's head. Richard was crazy and that's the way his mind really thought.

Richard not having sex with me contributed to Richard having sex with other females. At the time I didn't know about any other girls besides his other girlfriend Maria. But I knew if he was not having sex with me, he must have been having sex with a new chick. I say a new chick because that's just how it is with guys. Especially with guys that make money; they can afford the sex appetite and still make things right. They have their constants but then they have their variables too. Honestly, the way Richard was, I really believe that he was concerned with his penis touching the baby's head and that was probably his reason, but it also gave him an excuse to screw other females.

I stayed in Jersey most of my pregnancy but once I turned nine months I decided I was not staying in New Jersey anymore. I had already stopped going to school because it was too much. It was almost time for me to give birth and my doctor appointments became more frequent. Richard took me to my doctor appointments sometimes but not always. My stomach was getting bigger and bigger and it took a lot of energy traveling from New Jersey to the City.

I wanted to be closer to Mount Sinai Hospital on 99th Street and Fifth Avenue because that's where I had to go for my doctor appointments. I was almost nine months and I definitely did not want to go into labor while I was by myself in Jersey. I didn't want to take that chance, so I started staying with my friend Shelly at her mother's crib on 142nd Street in Harlem. Shelly lived right across the street from my foster mother's building.

February 23, 1988 was the day I found out Richard was cheating on me with a girl named Keda. Keda was from some housing projects in Harlem around 129th Street and 8th Avenue. I never knew about Keda and I never heard of a Keda until my friend Shelly told me about her.

It was my birthday February 23. I was at Shelly's mother's apartment all by myself. Shelly and her mother both worked in the evenings during the week. Shelly worked at a grocery store downtown Manhattan name Cristedes and I forget where her mother worked but I know she worked somewhere downtown also.

I didn't have any plans for my birthday, and I really didn't care. All I wanted was to hurry up and give birth. I was waiting for the baby to come any day.

Richard and I did not have a great relationship when I was pregnant. Most likely we were not speaking on the day of my birthday. I was very emotional when I was pregnant. I was always upset with Richard when I was pregnant.

I was sitting on the couch watching TV and it was my birthday and I had not spoken to Richard all day. It was already after eight.

The phone rang, I answered.

It was Shelly and the first words she said, "Did Richard call you?"

"No," I said.

Shelly paused, then she said, "He didn't call you for your birthday?"

"No and I don't care," I said.

Shelly said, "Well the only reason I'm calling you is because I don't think it's right that he did not call you for your birthday. I don't think it's right that it's your birthday and he is down here picking up this girl that works with me name Keda."

I paused and said, "Who is Keda?"

Was I hearing what I thought I was hearing? Richard was downtown picking up another female on my birthday. Richard hadn't even called me to say Happy Birthday. Even if we were not speaking, I would not have expected Richard to forget my birthday and be with another girl.

"Keda is a girl that works with me here at Cristedes," Shelly replied.

I was so hurt. My heartbeat dropped. I didn't know what to say. I was happy Shelly had to go back to work so I could cry by myself. I never talked about my feelings to others. I was always an introvert so whatever I felt I kept to myself.

I beeped Richard over and over again until he called me back.

"Where are you?" I screamed. "Where are you? You have not even called me to say happy birthday but you are downtown picking up some bitch."

I hung up the phone. Richard called me back. I picked up the phone and screamed, "Stop calling me and I'm giving this baby up for adoption." I hung up the phone again, Richard called right back. As soon as I picked up the phone he said, "I'm sorry, please don't give my baby away. I will take care of her."

I hung the phone up again. Richard kept calling me and each time I would pick up the phone and hang up. I was so hurt. I was in pain. I wanted Richard to hurt like I was hurting. I cried and cried. Richard finally stopped calling. I stayed balled up on the couch until I cried myself to sleep.

The next morning, I woke up to a phone call from Richard. "Get dressed and come outside." This time I did not hang up on him. I simply said, "Ok, I'm coming out."

By then, I had calmed down and I became extremely quiet. I was still hurt and didn't really know what to say.

I got dressed and went outside to meet Richard. It was early, around noon. He was driving a SUV. I can't remember what brand. As soon as I got in the car and closed the door, Richard drove off. I stayed quiet.

Richard said, "I'm sorry, I didn't mean to hurt you."

I responded, "Well you did. You hurt me a lot. You asked me to have a baby with you and I agreed, now I feel hurt and hopeless."

"I'm sorry," Richard said.

"It was my birthday. Do you know how I feel? It was my birthday and you was down at my friend's job picking another girl up. I'm hurt! Did you even remember it was my birthday?" I asked Richard.

Richard apologized and said, "Honestly Ang, I did forget it was your birthday. I was wrong."

I asked Richard who Keda was and he said that she was some girl from the projects. "Well, who is she?" I asked again.

Richard said, "She's nobody Ang."

"Well she must be somebody that you took the time to pick her up on my birthday." Richard didn't say anything because he couldn't say anything. I left the conversation alone because I was not going to sit there and force him to lie. Besides, Richard was not really a liar. Well in my opinion he wasn't a liar. I'm not saying he did not lie, what I'm saying is that he was more truthful than untruthful. We both knew the truth and that was that Richard was dating another girl and her name was Keda.

We went to Wilson's to have breakfast. Wilson's was on 157th Street and Amsterdam Avenue. While we were having breakfast, Richard gave me a box. "Happy birthday," he said. I opened the box and it was a Saint Barbara piece with diamonds in the crown, hanging from a Cuban link chain. It was beautiful and I will never forget it.

Richard apologized and bought me a beautiful gift for my birthday. It was more like a gift to ease the pain. I was still upset with Richard. He could have brought me the world and it still would not have settled the pain in my heart at that time. It was bigger than Richard cheating on me. Richard had asked me to have a baby. He asked me to be the mother of his child. I never wanted to have children early because of my own life experience but Richard made me feel safe and loved. After I got pregnant, I did not feel that way. I felt deceived and trapped.

I started spazzing out on Richard all the time after I found out about Keda. One time I was beeping him, and he did not call me back. I was at Shelly's apartment on 142nd Street. I beeped Richard a few times and he didn't call me back. So I got dressed, went to 142nd Street and 7th Avenue, flagged a cab down and told the cab driver take me to 132nd Street and 7th Avenue. I jumped out of the cab on the corner of 132nd Street and 7th Avenue. I remember it was dark outside so it must have been night time. I don't remember what time. Richard was standing with this chick name Sissy and a few other guys, his office cousin Red and a dude name Maurice. They was standing right in front of the garage. Richard's back was facing me as I walked down the block, he could not see me coming but I observed his friend Maurice telling him I was coming.

As soon as Maurice told Richard I was coming, Richard turned around. By that time I was right in his face. I was heated, so mad that I was beeping this nigga over and over again and he never called me back. But here he was with some chick in his face laughing and giggling with his friends. But he couldn't call me back. I spazzed out. I said, "So this is why you can't call me back!? Because you're around here with this freak bitch in your face!?" Sissy immediately left and walked down the block towards Lenox Avenue. In my mind, Richard got me pregnant and was taking advantage. Richard was not doing this shit before I got pregnant. Not calling me back, basically just ignoring me because clearly he could have called me back if he wanted to. Even not calling me on my birthday but picking up another chick from work on my birthday was disrespectful. I felt like I was at a disadvantage because I was pregnant. I couldn't go out and just fuck another nigger. I had too much respect for myself.

All I kept saying is, "Wait until I have this baby." Yes I wanted to hurry up and give birth so I could pay Richard back for cheating. I thought if he can cheat, I can cheat. I was planning on messing around with other guys just like he was messing around with other girls. I did everything to make Richard mad. I even went to the skating rink in New Jersey a week before I gave birth—BIG belly and all—I was there. I wanted Richard to find out.

Two and a half weeks later, on March 14, 1988, I gave birth to my daughter Reshonia Porter.

DADDY'S
LITTLE GIRL

⌒◦∞◦⌒

When I gave birth to my child, I didn't go into labor, my water didn't bust, I was three weeks overdue and scared. The doctor told me to come back on March 6, 1988 but I didn't go back to the hospital until March 13, 1988. I was feeling small pains and I didn't know what to do. I knew I was supposed to go back to the hospital on March 6th so I was extra paranoid. I was still staying with my friend Shelly. I had started back speaking to Helen, Yvette and Netta, so when I got scared to give birth, I called Yvette. Yvette had two children of her own. She was experienced and I thought she was the best person to call. I didn't call or beep Richard. I was still upset with him.

Yvette's brother from her father's side was visiting her when I called to ask for her assistance. So, he drove us to Mount Sinai hospital. When we got to the hospital Vinny wanted to go upstairs. In order for Vinny to be able to go upstairs with us he said he was the father.

I'm not sure how Richard found out that I was at the hospital, maybe Daniel told him, I don't know. But when Richard found out that I was at the hospital giving birth he came right away. When he got there, he could not come upstairs because the hospital already had Vinny on record as being the father. Richard was heated, as he should have been. Not that he was concerned with who was the father, but because someone was claiming to be the father and he could not come upstairs to see his baby be born. I was unaware of what went on until Richard told me once he got inside. I felt horrible because I didn't know Richard was at the hospital trying to get upstairs but I did know that Yvette's brother Vinny said he was the father in order to get upstairs to keep his sister company. And I didn't say anything, I just let it be done. So yes I felt horrible. I knew it was wrong but I never spoke up for myself when it came to my foster sister Yvette. Besides even though I was giving birth to Richard's baby I tried to act like I didn't care about him to my foster sisters. I was hurt and embarrassed that Richard was cheating on me. I had just turned nineteen years old, I was young, pregnant, emotional, and I was in love. I had no mother and no one with my best interest in mind. Sometimes people say they are helping you but, in reality, they have their own best interest in mind and not what's best for you.

After being in labor for about 10 hours, I gave birth to my baby girl, Reshonia, at 6:27 in the morning in Mt. Sinai Hospital on 99th Street in Manhattan. At eight pounds, four ounces and 19 inches long, she sure didn't look like a newborn. All it took was one look to see that she looked just like Richard. Richard was so excited when I gave birth, this was his first child and he couldn't stop smiling, he was bouncing around with so much joy. After having Reshonia, I was exhausted; I received a few pain killers and went to sleep. I opened my eyes back up around 11 am and Richard was standing in front of my bed with a big smile, flowers, and a brown bag. He came over and gave me a kiss. He put the brown bag down on the table and said, "Here, I got you some breakfast. I got you salmon cakes, eggs, and grits. I know that's your favorite." Richard knew I loved salmon eggs and grits—especially from Pan Pan's. Pan Pan was on 135th Street on Lenox Ave across from Harlem Hospital.

It was like he had ants in his pants the way he was bouncing around. Richard opened the bathroom door, not realizing it was being occupied by my hospital roommate who had also given birth. He was a mess, but a good mess. He came back over to my bed looking crazy. "Yo, why my daughter's head so big?" I looked at him and said, "Look in the mirror, there's your answer!" He laughed.

The nurse came in the room. "Hi, are you the dad?" she asked Richard. Richard said, "Yes, I'm the father." "Congratulations. She's scheduled for discharge tomorrow, there's some paperwork that has to be filled out. You two can fill it out tomorrow or you can go down and fill the forms out now." Richard said, "I'll go fill them out now, where do I go?" The nurse told him where to go and Richard went to fill out the forms.

When Richard was done, he brought the forms to me so I could sign them. The forms were basically his information as the father, my information as the mother and the name of our child. When he gave me the forms, I realized everything was filled out including our daughter's information—all I had to do was sign. I was happy Richard spelled Reshonia's name. I really didn't know how to spell it besides he named her so I figured he should be the one to spell her name.

Richard wanted a boy and of cause the name was going to be Richard. I wanted a girl but I decided if we had a girl I wanted Richard to name her. We talked about girls names a couple of times. It was January of 1988 when I was about 8 months pregnant. His mother called and told him his Aunt Janice had a little girl and her name was Tashana. Richard's aunt Janice was Richard's mother's youngest sister. As soon as Richard hung up the phone he said, "If we have a girl I want her name to be Rich-shonna. My Aunt Janice just had a little girl and her name is Tashana." We both agreed that if we had a daughter her name would be Reshonia and Richard would decide on how her name should be spelled.

After Richard finished with paperwork he left. It was Monday, so I knew Richard would be leaving soon. Mondays were always very busy for him. Monday was the day after the weekend, the first day of the week, the day to distribute the work, and the day to collect the weekend money. So yeah, I knew he was going to have to go soon.

Richard left and came back to the hospital later on to see us. It was around dinnertime, so he brought dinner for us to eat. It was soul food from Copeland's: smothered chicken, macaroni and cheese, and candied yams. He got himself the same thing from Copelands on 145th between Broadway and Amsterdam. Copeland's food was pretty good. Reshonia was lying in the hospital bassinet when Richard walked in the room. The nurse had just brought her to me about an hour before Richard came.

His energy was still the same, joy and happiness written all over his face. He put the food on the table and went to the bathroom to wash his hands. When he returned from the bathroom, he stared in the bassinet. "I can't believe I have a baby. Look at her. She looks just like me." Richard reached in his pocket and took out a jewelry box. In the box was a baby chain and bracelet. He put the bracelet on her and said, "This is to keep the wicked spirits away from her. I'll put the necklace on later." Richard put the necklace back in the box and put the box back in his coat pocket. He took off his coat and asked, "Can I pick her up?"

"Richard, she's your daughter."

"I'm scared, I don't want to drop her."

"Richard, pick her up," I said. "Just be gentle and hold her neck."

Richard picked Reshonia up. He could not stop smiling.

The next morning, it was time for us to go home. Richard came walking through the door. I was not quite ready, but Reshonia was ready to go. Richard had two Bloomingdale's bag in his hands.

"I got each of you an outfit to put on," he said.

"Richard, she is already dressed," I said.

"Nah, I want her to wear this. I'll change her clothes, you get dressed."

I agreed and went in the bathroom to get dressed. Richard got me an Adidas sweat suit with a pair of Adidas sneakers, so it really did not take me long to get ready. I came back out the bathroom and Reshonia was ready to go. She was dressed in a beautiful all-in-one winter white jumper, a little winter white hat that said "Princess," and a matching blanket which was laid out on the bed. Reshonia looked like an angel. I lifted Reshonia out of the bassinet and placed her on top of the blanket. I really didn't know what I was doing when it came to wrapping her but I had an idea. I wrapped her up as best as I could. "Here," Richard said, and passed me a beautiful Gucci baby bag. It wasn't really a baby bag—it was a big classic Gucci tote bag. It was already packed with diapers, baby lotion, bibs, and everything that a baby needed.

I waited to the main entrance of Mt. Sinai Hospital while Richard went to get his car from the parking garage. Richard pulled up in front of the hospital in his black 1988 535i BMW. "There's my boyfriend," I said to the nurse. I was sitting in the hospital wheelchair and the nurse wheeled me to the car. Richard got out of the car, came around to the passenger side, and opened the door. He took Reshonia out of my arms, I got in the car, he handed Reshonia to me, and closed the door.

In the back seat of the car were three bottles of champagne, a card, and a pink cigar box. I said, "That's nice, someone got you champagne and cigars." "Yeah. Last night I was celebrating. Me and a few fellas toasted to my baby girl. I asked Alpo to be the Godfather and he said yes." "That's nice that you made Alpo the Godfather." Although I did not like Alpo, I always respected Richard and Alpo's relationship. I knew Richard loved Alpo.

"Put your seat belt on," Richard said as he started the car. Reshonia stayed in my arms in the front seat. Back then, you were not required to have a car seat. Richard already had it in his head that he was taking his daughter straight to his mother at her apartment on 132nd Street. We started driving uptown. Richard took Madison Avenue and turned on 111th Street. He drove straight over to Lenox Avenue and made a right turn going uptown. We took Lenox Avenue uptown so Richard could stop and let his father Shelton see Reshonia. We stopped on 133rd Street, right in front of Lenox Terrace, in front of CandleLight. Candle Light sold Chinese food that was really good. I didn't go to the bar lounge but I always went to the Restaurant. Richard's father was standing there talking to some guys. As soon as he saw Richard pull up, Shelton walked over to the car. He bent down and looked through the passenger side window. "Look at my baby girl," Richard said. Shelton looked at Reshonia and smiled. "Congratulations, man. Congratulations to the both of you. Wow, she looks just like you. I know your mother is happy," Richard said. "Yeah, we about to go see her now..."

Before we got to Velma's house, Richard made a few stops to show his daughter off. I was looking forward to meeting Velma. I saw Velma a few times before and I would say Hi but Richard never formally introduced us. Richard would always be standoffish when it came to his mother at that time.

I don't think Richard was embarrassed of his mother because he didn't look down on anyone but he hated self destruction so, if anything, Richard was disappointed with his mother for being on drugs.

When I was pregnant with Reshonia, Richard told me his mother was in the hospital. By the time I gave birth to Reshonia, Velma was out of the hospital and Richard was with his mother everyday. Velma had got clean and was no longer using drugs. Richard was so happy and he was even happier to bring Reshonia home to his mother. When I first met Velma, I was a little timid. Velma had a strong personality, confident and bold. Almost like Jim Jones' mother, Mama Jones. Velma would talk shit behind my back and sometimes to my face but if I needed anything and she had it, then I had it. Velma was tuff on the outside but she had a heart like cotton candy.

Before we got to 132nd Street, Richard stopped at the number spot. The number spot was right on the corner of 131st Street and 7th Avenue. Richard stopped right on the corner and one of the number runners walk over to the car. "What you want?" the number runner asked Richard. "Give me 314, 804, and 627 for 10 dollars straight each, and five dollars boxed for each one." Richard played Reshonia's birthdate 314 March 14, her birthweight, 8 pounds and 4 ounces, and he played the time she was born, which was six twenty seven in the morning.

Richard took full responsibility for his daughter. He didn't want anyone else to do anything for her. I tried to get on WIC so I could get baby formula for free, paid for by the government. Richard said I couldn't get on WIC. Richard said someone else could fill that space because we did not need the free assistance. Similac was very expensive. Richard would go across the bridge to the Bronx to buy whatever I needed for Reshonia. Jetro was a wholesale store and Richard would go there and buy boxes of Similac baby formula, wipes, and pampers. He always made sure Reshonia had what she needed.

Richard loved shopping for his daughter, and everything he brought for her was the best. Velma would buy Reshonia clothes from the discount store and Richard wouldn't let Reshonia wear them. Richard would say, "Come on, Ma, I don't want my daughter to break out in bumps from this cheap material." Velma would say, "Oh please, Richard."

The best was all Richard knew. It was part of his DNA—quality all the time.

A THIN LINE
BETWEEN LOVE
& HATE

It was a before-and-after situation. Before I got pregnant, Richard and I were happily in love. But after my pregnancy, we were at war. Things got so bad we found ourselves pointing guns at each other. I hated Richard.

After I gave birth to Reshonia, I decided to stay back at my foster mother, Helen's house on 142nd Street. I didn't want to stay in Jersey, besides I was still in high school and needed the help. Richard hated that I chose to stay with Helen. He didn't like the way they treated me when I stayed with them. Some people that were from around the block, 142nd Street used to call me Cinderella.

He could not understand how everything was fine at first and then all of a sudden I was forbidden from seeing him. Richard took it personally and he did not like my foster mother or my foster sisters for that reason. He felt like they were jealous of me and did not treat me right.

It was true. When I first met Richard I was with my foster sister Yvette. She seemed to be excited that Richard and I had finally met in person. "Yes, that's my sister Angie!" She said it loud and proud.

Anyway I was embarrassed to be with Richard, well I was not really embarrassed to be with Richard, but I didn't want anybody to know that I still loved him so much. After he cheated on me with Keda on my birthday, I assumed everyone knew he was dating Keda including my "friends." At least that's what I thought. Shelly saw him picking her up on my birthday, how embarrassing. I was sure the whole block knew.

Keda was the first girl Richard really cheated on me with. Yeah I heard rumors about other females but they were just that, rumors, I had no facts. I already knew about Maria, but Richard and Maria's relationship never bothered me. And, Keda would not have bothered me either, it was the way it was done that hurt my heart.

In my mind everyone was looking at me like I was stupid. In my heart I was still in love with Richard. My inside world was in conflict with the outside world. And I decided to entertain the outside world leaving an empty feeling inside of me. I wanted my foster sisters to think that I no longer cared about Richard. I wanted the outside world to know that I was tough and I was not going to put up with Richard cheating on me. I was going to pay him back.

Reshonia and I spent a lot of time at Richard's mother's apartment when Reshonia was first born. Richard wanted Reshonia around him all the time. He definitely was not coming up to Helen's house to see her so he picked us up and dropped us on 132nd at his mother's house so he could spend time with her there. Velma loved every bit of it and so did Richard's little brother Donnell. Velma loved when Richard dropped us off because she was able to see Reshonia and she knew that meant Richard was going to be around all day. Richard spent a lot of time at his mother's house anyway but with Reshonia there that meant Richard was going to be there more.

Donnell loved seeing his little niece. Donnell always wanted to hold Reshonia and was never scared to hold her. One time I fell asleep on the couch while I was there. Reshonia was lying right in front of me, but when I woke up Donnell was holding Reshonia. He said, "My niece almost fell off the couch, but I caught her before she fell." He seemed a little annoyed, I understood and was thankful that Reshonia was ok.

I didn't have to stay around when Reshonia was at Velma's house but I wanted to. I knew that Richard was going to be in and out all day to see his daughter. I knew that if I stuck around, I would be able to keep an eye on Richard. I would stay at Velma's all day until I got my feelings hurt. Velma had a heart of gold but some of the things she said out of her mouth were crazy, and funny. One day I was at Velma's apartment with Reshonia. Velma went out and I fell asleep on the couch. Velma came in with her friend. As soon as you entered Velma's apartment the couch was right in your face and Velma's room was to the left. They had to pass by me. Their entrance woke me up but I still kept my eyes closed. When Velma and her friend got in her room I heard Velma tell her friend, " Yeah this bitch done set my son up." I stayed on the couch and thought, "What!" As soon as Richard came, I told him what his mother said and he laughed and said "Don't pay her any attention. She likes to gossip, she knows you didn't set me up." Richard was right. After being around his mother I realized that she didn't mean any harm, talking shit about people was just her character. Velma may have talked shit about me but she made sure I was straight. When Richard and I were not talking she took his money and told me to go shopping one day.

A couple months after I had Reshonia I was going to see this guy name Aron. Aron lived across the street from my foster mother. I used to deal with Aron way before Richard. I was probably fourteen years old when I dealt with Aron. And yeah I fucked him.

I did not deal with Aron for long but I thought he was ok. He asked me to come over. I said yes. I thought we was cool so I thought it would be ok. I had just had Reshonia so I was not about to have sex with Aron, that was not my plan. I was going through a lot and I thought Aron was a friend I could talk to.

I got dressed, went downstairs and walked across to his building. He lived on the first floor. I rang the bell, and when Aron opened the door, all of Richard's little flunkies from 132nd Street were there. I said, "Yo, you are a sucker," and left. Of course, they went back and told Richard. And even though I did not go in Aaron's apartment, the fact that I was obviously planning to, was enough. This nigga Aron had set me up. And yes, Richard was on fire.

Thirty minutes didn't pass before Richard was calling me on the phone. Richard called me up and was like, "Yo come to 132nd Street." I left Reshonia in the house with my foster sister and I went to 132nd Street. When I got to 132nd Street, Richard was standing there with some of the little guys from around the 132nd Street. I say little guys because they were usually the workers or the flunkies. Some of the guys that were standing with Richard were the same guys standing by the door in Aaron's apartment. I was like, "Oh shit."

I know Richard must've been embarrassed and hurt, because he felt the need to put me in the spotlight. Richard asked me in front of all the guys did I go to Aron's apartment. I wasn't about to lie. I was caught. I knew that when Aron opened his door. I said, "Yeah I went to Aaron's apartment but I didn't go in." What was you going over there for?" Richard asked. I couldn't say anything. I stayed quiet and Richard said, "Now you are on punishment, and you can't say nothing about Keda." Ok, so now I was supposed to openly accept him messing with Keda. I said, "Oh no, I'm not on no fucking punishment! Fuck you and fuck her! You can have her!" and walked away.

After that, Richard and I were broken up, departed, split—whatever you want to call it. I was like, fuck him, and he was like, fuck me. I was free to do what I wanted to do and I did just that.

Mother's Day came. It was my first Mother's Day. Richard and I were not on good terms but that didn't stop him from being the gentleman that he was. Richard called me up. He said, "I'm coming to get you, get ready, see if someone can watch Reshonia, tell 'em I will give them a hundred dollars." My foster mother agreed to watch Reshonia. Richard came to pick me up on 142nd. I have to laugh because it was Mother's Day. And I looked a hot mess when I think about it. I had on a jean skirt, a red Ralph Lauren polo shirt, and a pair of sneakers that were probably Reebok's. When I think about how I was dressed, all I can say is, I was young, and honestly, at the time, a t-shirt and jeans, or a sweat suit was always my thing.

I came downstairs and we drove to 132nd Street to pick up his mother, his aunt, and a few others. Some people met us at the restaurant. There were about 20 of us in total. We went to New Jersey to a really nice restaurant. It was on a nice boat. You could see New York City right across the water. The view was beautiful, you could look out into the Hudson and see the Statue of Liberty. It was nice. Richard and I went out on the deck. We looked through the telescope together. We looked at all the little boats in the ocean. My Mother's Day was so nice.

I enjoyed myself, but I could not wait to get back to Harlem. I had a date to go on. Richard and I were not together and I went on dates all the time, trying to fill the empty spot in my heart.

In the 1980s, a lot of guys were selling drugs and making money in Harlem. I never had a problem getting a guy or a date. I always seemed to attract the most generous guys. The guys back then never had a problem with spending money—taking a female out to eat or to the movies. That was part of the program if you wanted to eventually get the cat. And not only did the guys get dinner for the female they were dating, there was a good chance they were treating the entire household.

I really went on dates to try to make Richard mad.

But it never worked because the guys were always scared to let him see me with them. Me, honestly, I didn't care because I wanted Richard to know. I was hurt and I wanted him to be hurt.

I would even ask guys to drive me around 132nd Street to drop off our daughter at his mother's house. If they did drive me, they would drop me off a block away. They would ask me if I was fucking crazy. They were not about to fuck up their relationship with Richard for a piece of pussy.

So, Richard never really found out who I was fucking because they didn't want to fuck up their money, so they kept their mouths shut.

Well, there was one guy, Keith Sweat. Yes, Keith Sweat the singer. Keith used to hang out in an afterhour spot right next to my foster mother's restaurant. The afterhour spot was between 135th Street and

136th Street on Adam Clayton Powell Blvd on the downtown side of the avenue. I met him one Saturday morning when I was working at the restaurant. We exchanged numbers and went out a few times, but we never had anything serious and we never had sex. Keith was ok but I didn't like him. He had this cocky attitude about him. As if I was supposed to be happy that I was in his presence. He was wrong because I may have been quiet, but I always considered myself the prize. I liked Keith's song,s but I didn't appreciate having to listen to his songs every time I got in his car. Now I know that's what artists do, listen to their music all the time.

One time Keith called me up on the phone and he said, "Come on, we are going away." I asked, "Where are we going?" and Keith asked me, "Why should it matter if you are going with Keith Sweat?" I said, "It does matter." I told him I did not want to go. That was the end of the conversation and I hung up. I never saw or heard from Keith after that, and it did not matter. One thing about me is if I don't like a guy, I just don't like him. But yes, Keith was the only guy who ever drove me around 132nd Street. He had his own money, and he did not care if Richard saw him, because Richard had nothing to do with how Keith Sweat got his money. At least I don't think so.

I forget if Keith and I were going somewhere or what, but I know I asked him to take me to 132nd Street to drop Reshonia off and he said yes. He drove us to 132nd Street to Richard's mother's house. I was praying that Richard or someone would see me getting out of his car. I wanted Richard or someone he knew to see Keith Sweat bringing me to his mother's house to drop Reshonia off, but not a single soul was standing outside and no one saw. I was so disappointed!

When Reshonia was about 4 months, my foster mother Helen was watching her, and she rolled off the bed and hit her head on the night stand. I was in the kitchen. I heard Reshonia scream really loud. When I came out of the kitchen my foster sister Netta had already grabbed Reshonia up off the floor and was now in the living room. All I could see was blood gushing out of Reshonia's head. My foster sister Netta was there to help me. I panicked and could not do anything. Netta got Reshonia ready and we rushed out of the house, got in a cab and went to Harlem Hospital. Helen stayed home. Reshonia had to get four stitches in her head. When we got back from the hospital Helen said she was sorry. She said she did not expect Reshonia to move so fast. Richard was very upset that Reshonia fell off the bed while she was lying in the bed with Helen. He felt like Helen just didn't care enough. So when it came to people watching Reshonia, Richard didn't trust anyone.

One day I dropped Reshonia off at Richard's mother's house, Velma. When I walked in the door Richard was on the phone with this chick from uptown name Taytay. Richard and I were not together. I really didn't care that he was on the phone with her, besides she was fucking his cousin Daniel. Richard stayed on the phone. His workers were all sitting around the table bottling up with guns sitting in the middle of the table. "Who are you talking to, one of your bitches?" I asked. The chick must have heard me and said something about me having crooked teeth to Richard over the phone. Richard repeated it, "Yo, she said your teeth is crooked." I punched him right in his face and he slapped my face. I picked up one of the guns from the table and pointed it at Richard. Richard picked up a gun off the table and pointed it at me. We were by the front door. The guys got up from the table and ran to the back. Everybody ran out on the fire escape, even Richard's mother. We both looked into each other's eyes, and tears came to both of our eyes. I put the gun down and ran out the front door. I came back with my foster mother's brother to get Reshonia. When I got back, Richard was crying because he could not believe that I pointed a gun at him. I could not believe that he was allowing a bitch to disrespect me, and he had the nerve to tell me what that bitch said. The truth was that I was hurting; I honestly believe we were both hurting. Richard and I loved each other. The fact that I went to Aron's house really hurt him. The fact that he cheated on me when I was pregnant, hurt me. We were both hurt so we did things to hurt each other. Richard felt like me going to Aron's house made him look like a sucker. I felt the same way about him dating Keda and picking her up from her job and my friend witnessing it. Same shit. Hurt people hurt people.

Father's Day came around and I didn't even call him. I did not buy him a gift. I heard someone saw Richard sitting in his car on Father's Day looking sad.

The summer of 1988 was when Richard and I were really at war with each other. We were not talking, especially after our fight at his mother's house. We didn't call each other not even to talk about Reshonia. Well when I did call him, I would bother him about needing milk and pampers just to get on his nerves. I have to laugh because now I know I was very ghetto. "Richard! My baby need milk and pampers!" sounds real stupid today. One thing I can say is that Richard never entertained the stupidity. I guess he was saying you call me for milk and pampers but not to see my daughter. I got so mad at him and I tried to create even more of a reason for me not to let him see his daughter. Besides, I didn't stop Richard from seeing our daughter I just didn't make an effort to make sure he did see her and he didn't make an effort in my eyes to see her either. We both were being very stubborn.

Once in a while my girlfriend Dana would tell me that she'd seen

Richard when she had Reshonia. Dana's my friend from Harlem from the St. Nicholas projects. I met Dana after Reshonia was born, but Dana already knew Richard way before me.

After Reshonia was born and I started staying back with Helen, I started working back at the restaurant. Sometimes I would bring Reshonia to the restaurant and Dana would pick her up and take care of her while I worked. The restaurant was located on 125th and 7th Avenue and St. Nicholas projects are located on 129th and 7th Avenue. So, whenever Dana picked Reshonia up from the restaurant she would walk pass 132nd on her way back to the projects. Sometimes Richard would be standing on 132nd Street and 7th Avenue and he would stop Dana so he could see Reshonia. One time Dana said, "We saw her father today, he stopped us on 132nd Street when I was walking home. He didn't keep us too long, it seemed like he didn't want me on the corner with Reshonia."

If Richard saw Reshonia or not, Donnell his little brother always made it his business to see his niece. I remember the day I was standing on the corner of 142nd Street and Lenox Avenue. It was a nice summer evening. It was still light outside. Donnell and a few of his friends rode up on their bikes and surrounded me. I felt Donnell's energy was very serious at this time, he wanted to see his niece. Donnell said, "Where's my niece at?" "She's upstairs, you wanna see her?" Donnell answered, "Yeah." I went upstairs, got Reshonia, and brought her downstairs to see her uncle Donnell.

Richard not seeing his daughter didn't last long because I knew it was not right and, besides, if it did hurt Richard to not see his daughter, he acted as if it didn't. Richard had a lot of pride, and if something was hurting him, he never let it show.

Richard didn't go out to parties a lot, he didn't go roller skating and to the little clubs, so he would take Reshonia home a lot by himself. When Reshonia came back she was always well dressed but her hair was a complete mess, because her father would give her baths and her hair would get wet. I went out a lot, I went skating all the time, I went to parties all the time, house parties and clubs. Sometimes Richard would say he could not watch Reshonia just so I couldn't go out.

One day when Richard told me he could not watch Reshonia, I told Richard to let Kada watch Reshonia. He said, "I'm never letting another female be around my daughter." Richard always said he he would never have our daughter around another woman because they might pinch her or something. "Girls be jealous, they will be pinching my daughter and shit, nah, that's ok." I knew he would never have Reshonia around another woman because he always said that. I was just fucking with him when I said let Keda watch her. I didn't know this girl Keda and I would not have appreciated if he did let Keda watch my child. Still to this day if I seen her, I would not know, because I don't know what she looks like. Keda was not what really bothered me when it came to the situation. It was not about what was being done, it was about how it was being done.

I had friends that knew Keda, but I did not know her. I was way too cool to sit and ask questions or talk about another chick to anybody so I never learned anything about her. Once Richard and I broke up I was doing my own thing and he was doing his. We were tit for tat.

In the summer of 1988, I could not stand Richard and I'm sure he didn't like me either. He even stopped paying the rent for my apartment in New Jersey. One day in the summer of 1988 I went to my apartment in New Jersey and got a surprise. There was a padlock on the door. I was so embarrassed. I was with my foster sister Netta. Helen had a van for the restaurant that Netta drove. Netta was the only one with a license so I asked Netta to take me to my apartment to get some of my belongings. When we got to my apartment I could not get in because the door was padlocked. I called Richard, "Why the fuck is the door padlocked?" Richard said, "You were not staying there so I stopped paying rent, what you want me to keep wasting my money?" I was so heated, I cursed Richard out. "My stuff was in there, all of Reshonia things, my photos of my mother and us." Richard didn't say anything. Richard was not a person who argued that just was not his style. Honestly, I saw Richard raise his voice about two times. Sure, no more than three. I hung up the phone and that was the end of my apartment and my belongings that were inside.

Richard would make me so mad that sometimes I would just hit him for no good reason. Richard would just laugh and ask why I hit him. Richard was good at acting like nothing bothered him. He would make me mad before I would make him mad.

We'd had guns pointed in each other's face. That's definitely an example of a thin line between love and hate. Thank God no one got hurt. I was young.

WHAT IS MEANT TO BE WILL BE...

Richard and I started speaking to each other again when Reshonia turned one. Richard called me up and asked me if he could come get his daughter. I said yes. Richard came and got Reshonia from 142nd Street and Reshonia stayed with Richard on her first birthday.

Little by little Richard and I started communicating with each other in a meaningful way. We started going out on family dates, we went shopping for Reshonia together, and our conversations were purposeful. Eventually by the spring of 1989, we were back together. But this time it was none of anybody's business. I kept a lot of things to myself.

I was 19 years old, with a baby, still in high school. I was tired of going to high school so I decided to take my GED. I passed the GED test on the first try so that was it for me with high school. As soon as I got my GED, I got an opportunity for a receptionist position at Interboro Institute, an alternative school located on 56th Street between 9th and 10th Avenue. At Interboro a student can get their GED and earn college credits at the same time. It was one of the first colleges that you didn't have to already have a high school diploma that I knew about.

Ms. Bee referred me for the job at Interboro Institute. Ms. Bee was from 145th Street and 7th Avenue in Harlem. Ms. Bee was friends with a lady name Mrs. Klass. Mrs. Klass was the supervisor at Interboro Institute so Ms. Bee connected me to Mrs. Klass to schedule an interview. Ms. Bee knew me from around the neighborhood. She watched me grow up. Just about everyone knew my mother from the neighborhood and they knew she died. So that was part of the reason why Ms. Bee was looking out for me.

Before Interboro Institute, I was working in my foster mother's restaurant as a waitress. I had other jobs like summer youth jobs and I worked part time as a hostess at the Ponderosa Steak House when I lived in Nanuet, but this job was different. I was so happy. I hated working in the restaurant. I got paid a little something every week but it wasn't a lot of money. I hated that my hair and clothes always smelled like fish, chicken, and grease. So, I was real happy when I got my GED and I got my job at Interboro Institute. Plus, I got paid way more money than when I was working in the restaurant.

I was in an office setting, with my own desk and telephone. You could not tell me anything, working downtown in an office felt so good. I loved getting up every morning getting dressed up for work. It felt good walking to and from the train every day. The older men would always tell me, "You are a beautiful young lady." They always said that. I left things for the imagination because I always dressed conservative and never showed too much.

Richard loved that I was working somewhere other than my foster mother's restaurant. He hated that I worked in the restaurant period.

He felt like I should've been in college or working at a job that offered opportunities and allowed me to enhance my skills while learning new ones.

Our relationship was now going great. We started spending more time together with Reshonia and doing things as a family.

Richard and I talked about me moving from Helen's house, we discussed respecting each other wishes, we talked about sacrifice and the if's that come along with the risk that he took every day. We discussed what bothered each of us about the other. He told me what I did that bothered him, and I told him what he did that bothered me.

Richard didn't like me going out so much. He said, "Ang, you know I don't mind you going out, but you go out a little too much. You have a daughter now, you can't be going out all the time and leaving her with someone else to watch. You don't even want to come home with us, you'd rather go out to a party. I know you like to have fun, but now it's time to grow up."

He was right.

I told Richard that I hated when he did not call me back. There was so much going on at that time and if I beeped Richard and he did not call me back, I would get worried. I told him, "It's not just about you calling me back, it's about me wanting to know that you are okay." From that day on, Richard always called me back. No matter where he was, or whatever he was doing, he always called me back.

Richard said it bothered him when I would call him up saying, "Reshonia needs Pampers and milk." When Richard and I were not speaking, I harassed him by beeping him off the hook. Bugging him. "My baby need pampers and milk!" I would yell just to aggravate and try to control him. I felt like if I told him, "Pampers and milk," it would make him come right away, but it didn't.

Richard explained, "Come on Ang, you bothering me about Pampers and milk, it's not about the Pampers and milk. It's bigger than that. You mean to tell me if I'm not here, my baby not gonna eat, my baby not gonna have no Pampers? Ang, you know I will give you and Reshonia anything, but I wanna make sure if I'm not here you can take care of my daughter. My life is a sacrifice, anything can happen. I want to know that you and Reshonia are going to be okay."

One day we were sitting in the car, right in front of St. Nick projects. "So what's up with you and Keda?" "Keda gets on my nerves, she cries too much." "I heard we look alike." "Y'all don't look alike, I got pictures, I will show you what she looks like, we went to Disney Land together." "Oh, really?" "Yeah, you was doing your thing." Richard was right I could not say anything about what he was doing, and he could not say anything about what I was doing. Richard reached in the glove department of the car and took out a Disney envelope with pictures. He showed me a picture of Keda. I noticed Keda had acne and I said she doesn't look like me, she has bumps. Richard said, "Looks don't mean nothing Ang it's the person you are inside that makes you beautiful."

Honestly, I was hating and jealous.

Whatever bothered us, we acknowledged and discussed. We respected each other's wishes and agreed to solutions that would fix our relationship in a respectful way, as best we could.

After we got back together Richard told me he was expecting another child. The day he told me we were standing on 132nd Street, in front of the car garage talking. I remember it was May of 1989. "This girl from

Queens is having a baby from me." We had just started back talking so I was not upset. I was doing my thing and I was sure he was doing his. Getting another female pregnant was not a deal breaker when it came to my relationship with Richard.

Richard loved to shop, and he use to go crazy when he went shopping for his daughter. Reshonia had every outfit for her size for little girls that was in Bloomingdales. One time I was taking Reshonia to a little girl's birthday party, and I wanted her to wear a dress. Reshonia was around 18 months. I called Richard and asked him to pick her up a dress. He went and got her a dress from Saks Fifth Avenue and a few pairs of shoes from a little boutique shoe store inside Riverside Square Mall off of Route 4 in Hackensack, New Jersey. The dress and shoes were adorable. Unfortunately, though, the dress was over the top. It was a fairytale dress that would stand out in any crowd. It cost about $500. I couldn't let Reshonia wear the dress, she would have looked like the birthday girl, but better dressed. To keep the peace in the hood, I saved the dress for another occasion. Richard was always extra when it came to shopping for his daughter.

The summer of 1989 was the last summer Reshonia and I spent with Richard. It was a good summer for us. We spent time together and so did Richard and Reshonia. Reshonia was a big little girl, and she was always very smart. Reshonia was off the bottle before she was one, she was walking before she was one and she was using the bathroom before she was one. Reshonia was a big girl and Richard did not have a problem driving his little princess around with him in his drop top BMW. On a nice summer day Reshonia was his date. I remember the day Richard was bringing Reshonia back to me after taking her out for lunch and a ride. Richard pulled up on 142nd Street in front of Helen's building in his drop top car. Richard had his shades on and his cell phone sitting in his lap. I looked at Reshonia and she had her shades on and her toy cell phone that Richard brought for her, sitting in her lap. Reshonia loved to mock her father. Whenever he talked on his cell phone, she talked on hers, whenever he put his shades on, she had to put hers on. Reshonia knew her father was the shit.

Richard wanted to get me another apartment. I was fine with him getting me another apartment. I just didn't want it to be in New Jersey and I wanted something I could afford with or without Richard. I told Richard I applied for section eight and he said, "I don't want my daughter living in the projects." I explained to him that it was important for me to get something I could afford. I filled out for a few different housing opportunities but Richard would not agree to me moving into any subsidized housing program apartments.

One morning, when we were driving from Jersey, Richard and I were talking about life. It was a day in September 1989, the ending of summer and the beginning of fall. We were getting on Route 46 in New Jersey, heading to the George Washington Bridge going back to the city. Richard asked me, "What would you do if I get locked up?" I said, "If you go to jail, Reshonia and I will move to wherever you are, and we will come see you every week." Then he asked me, "What would you do if I get killed?" I told him I would jump out of the window. He said, "Don't say that," and I replied, "For real, I don't know what I would do without you."

Fall had now begun. It was October 1989 Richard, Reshonia and I were coming from his apartment in Harmon Cove when he told me, " I have another daughter, the girl from Queens had a girl, her name is Rhea. I probably can't have boys, they say some men can't make boys."

I'm not going to lie I don't remember what I said when Richard told me he had another child, but I do remember how I felt. I was happy for him.

In the fall of 1989 Richard took Reshonia and I on shopping sprees at Macy's, Bloomingdales, and Saks. Richard took us to little boutiques downtown because he always liked different things.

Right before Thanksgiving 1989, Richard got Reshonia this outfit from a little children's boutique named Morris Brothers on 84th Street & Broadway. He gave me the outfit to put on Reshonia. It was green. I guess it represented Thanksgiving, but then again, Hunter Green is a fall color. Anyway, it was a corduroy pants suit. I thought it looked a little boyish but rich. I got Reshonia dressed, and Richard came and took her to take pictures at Mr. Robs who had a studio set up in his apartment. When Richard brought Reshonia back to me, I took her coat, hat, scarf, and gloves off and that's when I saw the diamond name plate. I said, "Oh my God, look what daddy bought you." I beeped Richard and he called me back. "Oh my God, Richard, Reshonia's name chain is beautiful," I said. He said, "Yeah she took pictures with it on. Take it off of her and put it away."

Richard, Reshonia's and my last ride together was when we rode past some townhouses that were just being built. The townhouses are off of route 80 in New Jersey. Richard said "Let me show you where I'm moving my mother to, she doesn't want to leave 132nd but I'm moving her. I want all of my family out of Harlem it's too dangerous. " I said I want to move too but I just want something that is more affordable than the apartment he got for me in Cliffside Park. We were riding on Route 80, when Richard pointed the townhouses out to me. "There, right over there, you see those houses, that's where I'm moving my mother to." I don't remember the name of the townhouses, but I know it looked like they were still under construction, but you could tell they were going to be completed soon. That was the last time we all rode in a car with Richard.

COLD WORLD

T he day Donnell, Richard's little brother, was kidnapped, I had
just got home from work.

I got off from work at 5 o'clock, it was already dark outside.
A coworker of mine lived in Harlem, so we always took the A train
together. I would get off on 125th in St. Nicholas and walk through
St. Nick projects to 7th Avenue and walk to 142nd Street. I was still
staying at my foster mother's house. Sometimes, I would catch the C
or B train to 135th Street and walk from there, instead of walking from
125th Street. This night, I went to 135th Street & St. Nicholas Avenue
and walked home. It was rush hour and the train stations were crowded,
even the train on 135th Street and St. Nicholas had a lot of human traffic
during rush hour, so I felt safe.

As I walked home, the blocks seemed to be quiet, and the evening
seemed to be gloomy. I could feel the energy in the air. I could feel
that something was wrong. When I got around my block, the corner
was empty. That was unusual; yeah, it was cold outside, but even in the
winter, somebody would be on the corner, a drug dealer, a lookout man,
or a drug user. But not this night—nobody was outside.

When I got upstairs and inside the apartment everyone was home. Yvette, Helen and Netta were in the living room. I noticed the energy seemed a little weird. I took off my coat and picked up Reshonia to say hello, like I did every day. I went in the kitchen to wait by the phone just in case Richard called because normally he called me when I got home from work. The phone rang, I picked it up but it was not Richard, it was my friend Nia. As soon as I said hello she noticed my voice and said, "Angie, you heard what happened to Richard's little brother Donnell?" I said, "No, what happened?" My friend said, "Somebody kidnapped Donnell, nobody told you?" "No, nobody told me, oh my God." "They said the kidnappers cut Donnell's finger off and sent it to the McDonald's on 125th Street and Broadway, I heard Daniel was the one who went to get the finger from McDonalds. Yvette and them didn't tell you?" "No, nobody told me, let me call Richard now. "

As soon as I hung up the phone, I beeped Richard. It was less than a minute before the phone rang. I picked the phone up hoping that it was him. It was Richard, I could hear it in his voice when he said hello, that he was really upset and on the verge of crying. I told him that I had heard about Donnell. Richard said, "Yeah, it's fucked up. I'm on my way around there to see you now, I'll talk to you when I get there."

When Richard came upstairs, I came out to the hallway. Reshonia was in my arms. I closed the door behind me. He stood with his back against the wall, facing the stairways. Richard had one foot flat against the wall and a toothpick sticking out the side of his mouth. Richard waved his knee back and forth.

"This shit is crazy Ang. Who the fuck cuts off a little boy's finger. These niggas are crazy. Ang, I don't know what's going on." Richard sounded like he wanted to cry. His voice was shaky, and he kept saying this shit is crazy over and over again. I didn't know what to say. What could I say to Richard? His little brother had been kidnapped. His little brother's finger had been cut off and sent to McDonald's. Richard blamed himself. I know he blamed himself because he said to me, " Ang I know if this was Reshonia you would kill me." I couldn't say anything because I really don't know what I would have done if the kidnappers had taken Reshonia. In a situation like this you can't say what you would do unless it happened to you. Richard did not know who kidnapped his brother Donnell. All I could do was listen. I did not know what to say.

Richard told me that they informed the police and the kidnappers stopped calling as soon as the police got involved. "The kidnappers were communicating with us, calling my mom's house, but as soon as we got the police involved, they stopped calling. That's when they sent a letter to my Aunt Joanne's apartments uptown in Dykeman, Daniel's mom." "What do you mean they sent a letter? Who sent a letter? How did your aunt get the letter? What did the letter say?" "It said for me to go to the bathroom inside of McDonald's on 125th street on Broadway, some Puerto Rican lady gave my Aunt Joanne the letter from the kidnappers." "Who was the lady?" I asked. "I don't know they said they opened the door for her, and she gave them the letter and left." "What happened?" Richard said, "Daniel went to McDonald's, and when he got there he found a brown bag." I couldn't hear anymore, I started to cry. Richard did not continue with the details it was too much hurt and pain for him to describe and too much for me to hear.

I never really understood that part. How could some bitch just come and drop off a letter without someone grabbing this bitch in and questioning her?

It should have been a one-for-one. You have Donnell—and I have this bitch.

All types of shit were going through my mind. Honestly, I still believe in my heart that more of Richard's family were involved with kidnapping Donnell, besides his uncle.

Richard took his foot down off the wall and took Reshonia out of my arms. He told her he loved her and told her to give him a kiss. Reshonia looked at Richard and gave him a kiss and a hug. Richard gave Reshonia back to me.

He started pacing back and forth. "Ang, I don't know what to do. I feel so bad, my mother is going crazy. This is all my fault." I was speechless. Richard gave Reshonia a kiss again. I took her inside and put her in her playpen.

I came back out and gave Richard a hug. We held each other for about 20 minutes, we both started to cry. Richard gently pushed himself away from me, wiped his eyes and then wiped mine.

Richard said, "I'm going to call you in a little while," and walked down the stairs. I stayed in the hallway until I heard the building front door close.

After Richard left, I went back into the apartment and put Reshonia in the tub, and I sat on the toilet just thinking. Tears started rolling down my eyes. What's going to happen next? I sat on the toilet looking at Reshonia and praying to God. How could someone cut off a child's finger? This drug shit was really serious.

The next morning, I got up and went to work. I stopped at the newsstand to get the newspaper. I always purchased the Daily News, but this morning I could not help but notice the front page of the Post. All I remember seeing was the word, "Kidnapped."

When I got to work, the first thing I noticed was the newspaper on my coworker's desk. It was the New York Post, Donnell's picture on the front page. My heart started to race. I didn't say anything; I couldn't say anything. I never told anyone at work my business, so they didn't know that Richard was my daughter's father.

I went to work every day after Donnell was kidnapped because I felt in my heart that something else was going to happen. I knew that I needed to keep working so that I would be able to take care of myself and my daughter. Besides, I wanted Richard to be able to get the money to get his brother back and not worry about taking care of me and Reshonia. It was time for me to step up and do what I had to do.

It was a really scary time for me. It was winter, and when I got off from work, it was already dark outside.

One night, I was walking home from work, down 140th, between Lenox and 7th Avenue. This guy was walking across the street toward me, and he put his hand in his coat. My heart dropped and I ran down the block.

Another time, I got a phone call. It sounded like it was a male's voice. The caller said, "Rich can't get the money for his brother, let's see if he can get the money for his daughter." I don't know if they were serious or not but I damn sure took it seriously. I was scared. I remember looking out the kitchen window and seeing a car drive by with a bright flashlight shining up at the window. I was paranoid and scared.

Richard and I talked on the phone every night. Richard told me over and over again that once he got his brother back, we were moving out of

New York. "I have land in Florida, and we are moving to Florida. Me, you, Reshonia, and Donnell. We are out of here." I never said anything to Richard, but I was scared. And even when he asked me to move to Florida with him—that scared me too. I have always been intuitive and I saw this coming. Let's be real. They kidnapped a little boy and cut off his fucking finger in the same day—who the fuck does that? These weren't regular caring human beings.

It was around Christmas time, Richard asked me what I wanted for Christmas. Then he asked me what I wanted him to get for Reshonia. I just looked at him in shock. I was shocked that he would even be thinking about Christmas when his brother was missing. And I was annoyed that Richard did not know me better than that. Don't get me wrong. I love Jesus Christ and all of that but fuck a Christmas gift when Donnell was missing.

I said, "Richard your brother is missing, and he is more important than any Christmas gift." I couldn't understand why he would be worried about a Christmas gift. Besides, who would feel right accepting a Christmas gift from him right now.

Richard was a giver and, if anything, it was time to give to him.

All the motherfuckers in Harlem who claimed to be making money that he looked out for.

I could never understand why his so-called friends never came together to get the money up for him to get his brother back. Everybody claimed that they were making money.

Anyway, I told Richard that Christmas did not need to happen that year.

Christmas came and went, and Donnell still wasn't home. The kidnappers took Donnell right after Thanksgiving on December 5th. It was almost a month since Donnell had been kidnapped.

Richard told me they lowered the ransom from $500,000 to $250,000. Richard kept saying that, as soon as he got his brother back, we were moving to Florida. Lord knows I wanted to tell him to leave right then and there. I just kept wondering what was next. But I couldn't and I would have never told him to leave without his brother.

Richard cried many nights on the phone with me as he took the blame for Donnell being kidnapped. We would listen to Anita Baker and Allison Williams. He loved Allison Williams' song, "Just Call My Name." Our last nights were spent on the phone. I would sit in the kitchen, up on the counter, right by the phone, waiting on his phone calls every night when I got home from work.

THE LAST CALL

I will never forget the last time I heard Richard's voice.

The date was January 3, 1990.

"I'm going to call you back, I'm going to call you back."

January 3rd was a Wednesday, it was the middle of the week. Hump day. I had to go to work that day, actually everyday was hump day since Donnell had been kidnapped. I got up that morning and went. When I got off, I went straight home.

It was the same routine every day. When I got home from work, I fed Reshonia dinner, bathed her, gave her some tender loving care, read her a bedtime story, and put her to bed. Reshonia was asleep every night by 8:30pm.

This night started off no different.

Reshonia was asleep by 8:30pm, and I was in the kitchen waiting on my nightly phone call from Richard. Richard usually called me around 9:30pm, the same time every night. We talked and shared how our day went. We checked in on each other's mental health, we talked about Reshonia, and we discussed getting Donnell back. There was never a night that I spoke to Richard that I could not hear the pain in his voice. There was never a night that he gave up, he was always so optimistic about getting his brother Donnell back. Every night Richard apologized, "Ang, I'm so sorry, once I get my brother back, we outta here. Me, you, my daughter, and my brother. We moving to Florida. I got land in Florida. As soon as I get Donnell, we leaving." This night was the same. Richard reiterating his plans for us. We wished each other a good night and hung up.

When we hung up, it was around 10pm.

About an hour later I was lying down, and I heard the phone ring. I always listened for the phone to ring to see if it was Richard calling for me. Even if it was after we said goodnight to each other. Sometimes, Richard would call me back just to talk. I always listened. I wanted to be there for Richard at all times. I wanted to make sure no one made the mistake of ever thinking I was asleep. My foster sister Yvette answered the phone, and I heard her say, "Hold on." She came to the bedroom door and told me that Richard was on the phone for me. I was lying down on the bed with Reshonia next to me. I got up and went to the kitchen to get the phone. The first words that came out his mouth were, "Let me speak to my daughter." He sounded anxious, under pressure, and pressed for time. I said, "Richard, it's late. You know Reshonia goes to sleep early. Hold on, let me see if she's up." It was around 11pm and she was already sleep. Richard knew Reshonia went to sleep no later than nine o'clock. But, because of the circumstances, I checked anyway. I put the phone down on the counter and went to see if Reshonia was up. I cut on the light in the room she was sleeping. I was hoping the light would wake her up, but her eyes remained shut. I touched her softly and quietly said her name. She didn't blink an eye or move a limb. She was in a deep sleep. I went back to the phone and told him she was asleep.

Richard said, "I'm going to call you back. I'm going to call you back. I'm gonna call you back." Three times he said he was going to call me back. I knew something was not right. The tone in his voice was different. The speed of his words just wasn't right. Something wasn't right. I felt it in my heart. First of all, Richard never called and just requested to speak to his daughter. That was odd. Don't get me wrong. Richard would talk to Reshonia on the phone all the time, but that was not how the dialogue usually went. I knew something was not right.

I hung up the phone. My mind was racing. I waited for Richard to call me back. About 30 minutes passed and I still had not heard back from Richard. This was definitely out of the ordinary. Richard and I had an understanding and he always called me back if he said he was going to call me back or if I beeped him. Even if he was on top of a bitch, he would still call me back. And the fact that he repeated three times that he was going to call me back. Those were key words. He was definitely trying to tell me something was not right. I picked up the phone to call him. I punched in Richard's beeper number. Actually I can't remember if I was going to beep him or call his cell phone but either way it did not matter because the house phone was disconnected. I thought, "Damn, the house phone was just working." It was weird that the phone company would disconnect the phone after 11pm.

I knew something was wrong. I wanted to go downstairs to use the payphone, but I was scared. Something was wrong I knew it and I was right. I didn't feel like I had anyone to talk to, my foster sisters and my foster mother despised Richard's and my relationship. I lay down in the bed, in a fetal position. Reshonia was lying right in front of me. I put my arm around Reshonia and held her firmly like she was my pillow. It was very hard for me to go to sleep. Richard was on my mind and I was worried. When I finally fell asleep, I had a terrible dream. A monster was in the window. I lay in bed facing the window. The monster was right in front of me, hovering over me and laughing. It was big and its body was halfway in the window. I couldn't see his feet, but his face and upper body reminded me of a reptile. It was so crazy, it was laughing hard at me.

I remember fighting to open my eyes. When I finally opened my eyes, the monster was gone. I couldn't go back to sleep. I lay in the bed until it was time for me to get ready for work. As soon as 7:00am hit, I jumped up and went to the bathroom. I ran my bath water and got in the tub. The whole time I was in the tub, Richard stayed on my mind. "I'm going to call you back." Those words replayed in my head over and over again.

I got out of the tub, wrapped a towel around my body and went back to the room. When I got there, Reshonia was up. That was the norm for her. Every morning, she watched me get ready for work. I gave Reshonia her breakfast. That morning she had microwave pancakes and link sausages. I put her serving table in front of her with the pancakes and sausages on it. Reshonia fed herself while I got dressed. By the time I was finished getting dressed, Reshonia was finished eating. I wiped her off and sat her on the potty. "Pee pee mommy!" Reshonia exclaimed. That's what Reshonia would say when she wanted me to know she was done. That was her way of letting me know she handled her business. I took Reshonia off of her potty, got her dressed, and put her in her play pen in the living room. I cut the TV on, turned to Sesame Street, gave my baby a kiss, and left for work.

That morning, I did not stop for nothing. I could not wait to get to work so I could call Richard. I walked to 125th so I could catch an express train to 59th Street. It was cold outside, but I always chose to walk to 125th Street train station because there were more people around. I could have taken the local train on 135th and St. Nicholas, but at that time, I was still very afraid and the 135th train station was too quiet and that scared me.

As soon as I got to work, I called Richard mother Velma's house. I can't remember if I called his cell phone first. I called his mother's house, and Richard's sister answered the phone. I asked, "Where is Richard? Because he didn't call me back last night."

"It's true, they found him dead," Pat said.

I said, "They found Donnell?"

She paused for a second, "Where are you at?"

I said, "I'm at work."

She said, "Nobody told you? They found Richard dead."

Richard's sister sounded sad. I guess she assumed I already knew that Richard was dead when she said, "It's true they found him dead." She seemed shocked that I did not know. When she said it's true they found him, maybe she thought I knew because her cousin Daniel was my foster sister Yvette's man and we lived in the same house. I didn't know who knew what, all I knew was my daughter's father got killed and I was devastated.

I dropped the phone and all I can remember is being back at my foster mother's house crying. Later, I learned that I passed out and my supervisor, Ms. Klass, called my foster family. My foster sister Netta came to get me from work.

When I got back to my foster mother's house, I stayed in the bed room crying non-stop. I cried and I cried. Every time I put something in my mouth, I would vomit. I felt like I was dying. I couldn't breathe and it felt like there was a knot in my throat. I was gasping for air and drowning in tears. I just could not stop crying. I kept asking myself, could I have done something to help him? He was clearly under pressure. My mind was going crazy trying to figure it out.

Richard knew he was about to get killed when he called to speak to his daughter. I could tell there was a gun in his back when I picked up the phone and he demanded to speak to his daughter. Well maybe he didn't know he was about to get killed but whatever was going on he was under pressure.

Maybe the killer let Richard have that one last phone call. I believe Richard asked for the phone call. He loved his daughter, and everyone knew that. Reshonia was only 22 months old. When Richard was killed, my whole world shattered. I was only 20 years old and I felt like he abandoned me. I later realized Richard did not abandon me. He knew his life was a sacrifice and he trusted that if something were to happen to him, I would be able to make it on my own. Richard was right.

WHO KILLED RICH?

Who killed Rich and left his body at the front entrance of Orchard Beach? Like it was trash.

Orchard Beach is a landmark in the Bronx. It's filled with tasty seafood restaurants, and a nice beach with beautiful boats and yachts.

But for me—it's where Richard was left after he got killed.

Yep, his body was found near the woods on the side of the road on Orchard Beach. Multiple shots to his body and a shot to the head. Clearly, the person who killed him wanted to make sure he was dead. It was not hard to tell whoever killed Richard was full of jealousy, envy, a wicked spirit, and a heart filled with hate. The person dumped him off like garbage. I guess they were trying to make a statement and down play him by throwing him out on the side of the road.

Donnell was still missing. Somewhere with his finger cut off. Richard was in the streets trying to get the money up to get his brother back. It was the perfect opportunity for a coward to try to make a slick move.

Harlem was in a state of shock. Everyone was talking about Richard getting killed and wondering what was to come next. His killer started a ball of confusion and knew it. Who killed Richard?

Was it the same people who kidnapped Donnell? I knew it wasn't them, and I was sure everyone else knew it, too. Why would they kill Richard before getting the money? I'm sure they were planning on killing Donnell and Richard once they got the money—it's fucked up—but it obviously would have served them no purpose to leave either of them alive.

Drip didn't waste no time coming to see where his money was at. Well, he didn't come, but he sent a girlfriend of his to see me. Drip was the guy Richard got his drugs from. Reshonia and I were at my foster mother's apartment. My foster sister Yvette came in the bedroom where Reshonia and I slept. She said Taya wants to talk to you. She's in the front by the door. I knew Taya from this girl, Kia, who was a friend of a friend. Kia and Taya sold drugs together. Taya wanted to know if I knew where Richard's black book was. Richard kept track of everyone he distributed work to inside of a black book, and I guess Drip noticed. Written by each person's name was the date, the amount of cocaine he gave to each person, how much they owed, and the due date.

Taya said Drip had given Richard 40 keys of cocaine to help get Donnell back. He sent Taya to find out where the 40 keys was at or where the money was at.

Taya said Richard told Drip that he was moving us to Florida, so Drip figured if anyone would know anything about his business, it would be me. I told Taya I didn't know anything. I really didn't know much. I knew Richard had the black book and I knew that he kept a record of his business transactions in the book but I did not know where the black book was.

About an hour after Taya left, the FEDS came to my foster mother's house. They knew I was there because that's the address I used for everything. Two male detectives, one was white and the other one was black. They wanted to talk to me because they knew Richard and I had a child together. I came out of the bedroom and sat on the couch. The detectives remained standing. They asked me a number of questions and my answer was always "no" or "I don't know." I don't remember all of the questions they asked me, but I do remember feeling like I was being interrogated. They asked me if I knew about Richard messing around with other girls. They asked me if I knew Keda. I told them no I didn't know about any other girls. My foster mother lifted her voice and said, "Yes you do." I didn't say anything. "Why are you lying, you know Keda, my foster mother or my foster sister," Yvette said. I can't remember which one of them said it. The detectives asked me a few other questions and I answered "no" or "I don't know" to everything. I don't remember any other questions besides the questions the detectives asked me about other girls. And that's because I remember feeling like they were trying to see if I was some jealous baby mother playing a part in getting my child's father killed. I could care less about a bitch. The love of my life and the father of my child was dead. Another female was the last thing I wanted to talk about.

One of the detectives handed me a card and said, "Here's my information. If you need anything, call us. I'm really sorry for your loss. Right now, Mr. Porter's possessions are being gathered together and whatever is not confiscated belongs to you. Everything goes to his daughter as she is his next of kin, and because she is still a baby, everything will go to you."

I really didn't care about getting Richard's possessions. All I could think about was the fact that my daughter's father was dead.

His family sold most of his stuff anyway. His cars, his jewelry, his fur coats—they even tried to sell his story.

Neither my daughter nor I benefited and it was all right, because there was nothing Richard left more valuable than his daughter. In my mind, I held the golden egg.

The FEDS left, and I went downstairs to go to the corner store. When I got downstairs, everyone was standing in front of the store on Lenox Ave. This guy named Deon said, "Come here Ang." Deon was another drug dealer from 142nd Street. Deon was talking to Black Jus on his cell phone. I had never formally met Black Jus, but I knew he was one of Richard's friends. Deon handed me his cell phone. "Hello?" He said, "Hi Ang, this is Black Jus." I said, "Hi, Jus." He said, "Be careful. Just be careful." That was all I remember him saying. I believe that Black Jus was looking out for me, but he really made me scared. He said it very intensely. After I was done talking to Jus, I went back upstairs. Actually, I didn't go downstairs to go to the store. I just wanted to get out of the apartment after my foster mother and foster sister's had gotten on my nerves when the FEDS were there.

When I went back upstairs, I went straight into Netta's bedroom. Reshonia and I slept in my foster sister Netta's room because Netta stayed at her boyfriend's apartment most of the time. I could not stop crying— my face looked like the elephant man. My eyes were so swollen, when I looked in the mirror, I didn't recognize myself.

Why? Why me? Why would God give me this life?

If it wasn't for my daughter, I don't know what I would have done.

The phone rang, it was Velma—Richard's mother.

Velma called to ask me if I knew where Richard's money was. She said she knew that if Richard confided in anyone, it would be me. I did not know where any money was. I told her that he may have some money in his safe. Richard had a safe inside of his china closet in the dining room. The key was on the top of his headboard in his apartment in Secaucus. Before Velma hung up, she asked me if I was ok, I quietly mumbled yes as I started to cry. I hung up the phone and went back into the bedroom.

Who killed my daughter's father!?

I could not stop crying. I lay in the bed with my face in the pillow. Reshonia lay right next to me. My foster sister Yvette came to the bedroom door. The door was slightly open. She raised her voice and yelled through the door, "I don't know why you're crying that was not your man." How could someone be so mean and say something so hurtful. I was already in so much pain and for her to have no compassion and say what she said. How could she be mad at me for being hurt because my child's father was dead and gone? Normally, I didn't say anything back to her but this time I was not going to let it go. I got up from the bed and I yelled back at her. I forget exactly what I said. I know I started blurting out all types of disrespectful things that I knew Daniel did to her. Yvette and I started to fight, my foster mother came, it became a big fight and to me it seemed like it was them against me. My foster mother was very protective of Yvette's relationship with Daniel. She did not allow anyone to ever tell Yvette anything that Daniel did, anything that would hurt Yvette or her relationship with Daniel.

After the fight, I was not about to stay at Helen's house. I grabbed

Reshonia and a few things and we left. I forgot if I called Velma or Pat, I don't remember how they found out about the fight. I just remember Pat standing down the steps telling me to come on. I remember someone telling me to leave Reshonia there because I could not take care of her. I was like, "Hell no, I'm not leaving my child."

Reshonia and I went to Velma's apartment on 132nd Street until I figured out my next steps. Richard was gone and I didn't have any blood family, so I had to figure out where Reshonia and I was going to live. I knew it wasn't a problem for Reshonia to stay at Velma's apartment but where was I going to stay? I'm sure Velma would have let me stay with her, but I wasn't comfortable staying at Velma's apartment.

This was the first time I ever met Pat. I asked Richard about his sister all the time and he would say she did not like to leave Azie's mother's house. Richard did not like his sister staying at Azie's mother's house. He did not like Pat and Azie's relationship. Richard used to say he wished his sister would leave off of the hill and come see her family. The area that Azie's mother lived in is call Sugar Hill. Richard believed it was because of Azie that Pat did not come see her family. He was concerned that she was unhappy and not being treated right by Azie's family.

Richard was upset one time because he said Pat had a fight with some girl inside of Azie's mother's house. He did not like that at all and whoever the girl was, he didn't like her either. Pat only saw Reshonia when Velma took her up to Azie's mother's house to see her.

As soon as Reshonia and I got to Velma's apartment, we went straight into her bedroom. There were a few people in the apartment, I can't remember everyone that was there, but I remember his Uncle Johnny and Daniel was there. They were standing to the right in front of the stove, right by the bathroom. I went left through the living room and straight to Velma's room. I noticed a few people sitting on the couch, but I didn't get a good look at their faces. My eyes were filled with tears. Everyone and everything looked like a big blur.

Velma was in her room, she took Reshonia out of my hand and undressed her. I took my coat off and laid it on the chair in Velma's room. I sat at the edge of the bed, Velma lay Reshonia in the middle of the bed. I stared up at the ceiling, silently talking to God. I was in such disbelief.

That night, I stayed at Velma's until Reshonia went to sleep. After Reshonia went to sleep, I went to Shia's and Nia's mother's apartment on 140th Street, Mrs. Laura. I didn't bring Reshonia with me to Mrs. Laura's house because there was limited sleeping space. I was always able to find a space to sleep whereever I was at but I did not want to have to worry about Mrs. Laura having to make space for the both of us. And I didn't stay at Velma's place because it was too many people there, I was more comfortable with my friend's Shia and Nia.

The next morning, I got up, got dressed and went back to Velma's apartment to be with my baby. When I got to Velma's apartment, Richard's sister Pat was getting the funeral arrangements together. She was also writing Richard's obituary. The viewing and funeral were to be held at Bentas Funeral Home on 141st and St. Nicholas Avenue. Richard's body was to be buried in New Jersey at Holy Trinity Cemetery. I did not agree with what the obituary said but I didn't make a big fuss. However, I do remember it saying that Richard was leaving behind his loving fiancé Maria and his love and companion Keda. I thought that was stupid, not because they left me out but because it was just stupid. I said to Pat if you are going to put this bullshit in his obituary you need to make sure his other daughter is included. You have a fiancé and a love and companion?

Damn that was adultery before they even got married. I never really cared about anyone including me, I didn't need any validation.

After the arrangements were made, I left and went back to 140th Street, to Shia and Nia's apartment. There were a lot of people visiting Richard's family at Velma's house. I did not like to be around a lot of people that I did not know, so I stayed with Reshonia for most of the day, then I went back to 140th Street to Shia and Nia's mother's apartment. Reshonia stayed with Velma.

The day of the viewing was very sad. I felt like I could not breathe. I felt like I was suffocating, and I had a knot in my throat that would not go away. My heart was broken. My mind was cloudy, and the tears constantly continued to roll down my face. I was with a female from Harlem, Connie. I did not know Connie until after Richard got killed. She stopped me when I was walking down 140th Street going to Shia and Nia's. She asked me if I was ok. I said yes. She gave me her beeper number and told me to beep her later. After that day we became friends.

The day of the viewing Connie came to get me from Shia and Nia's mother's apartment on 140th street. I don't remember exactly what happened but I remember Connie came to get me and she took me shopping. We went downtown to Madison Avenue. Connie wanted to make sure I looked the part for Richard's funeral. We went to a few boutiques on Madison Avenue. She picked me out an outfit that she thought was beautiful for me to wear. I was out of it and nothing really mattered. I didn't care what I wore to the funeral. Connie was determined to dress me up and that's what she did. She bought me a beautiful black dress, and a nice pair of heels. She even got me a real Blue Fox fur coat to wear. Accessories were a necessity for Connie. She made sure I had a hat, a nice pocketbook, fancy gloves, and costume jewelry.

After we were done shopping, we headed uptown to the viewing. Connie suggested we get something to eat. She asked me what I wanted to eat. I told her I wasn't hungry. She told me I had to eat something, and she knew this really good Chinese restaurant right on 96th Street and Broadway. I ended up getting my food to go. I started to cry more and more. I believe just knowing that we were getting closer and closer to viewing Richard's body gave me anxiety. My heart began to hurt, it became hard for me to breathe again. I knew anxiety was causing the pain in my chest.

Connie pulled up in front of Bentas Funeral Home on 141st Street and St. Nicholas Avenue. There were cars everywhere. Cars were double parked from 141st Street to 145th Street on St. Nick, both sides of the Avenue. Cars were pulling up in front of the funeral, guys and gals were jumping out, going inside to view Richard's body. There was a lot going on and I just couldn't handle it.

Besides, in my mind—everyone was suspect.

I told Connie I couldn't go in, I felt like I was about to die so I waited in the car. Connie went inside of Bentas and within fifteen minutes she came back out, got in the car, and drove me to 140th Street back to Shia and Nia's apartment.

The funeral was the next day.

I went, but I honestly don't remember a thing. The most I remember is pulling up to the funeral home with Connie. It was like a car fashion show. Everyone looked so nice. It was winter and everyone had on their best outfits; minks, shearlings, and all sorts of fur coats was all I saw. Everybody's face was a blur, so I can't recall anyone. Cars were lined up all on St. Nicholas Avenue; Benzes, BMWs, Four Runners, Porsches—it was a sight to see. Everybody pulled up when Richard got killed. There was so much respect.

Connie parked the car, got out, and opened my door. I got out of the car, Connie took my arm, and escorted me in the funeral home. I remember sitting down. I remember being a few rows behind the family. I remember trying to avoid looking toward Richard's casket. However, I remember a flashback that turned black as soon as I looked towards casket and saw Richard's face. That's all that I remember about Richard's funeral. If my body was at the burial, my mind definitely was not, because I have no recollection of seeing Richard get buried at all.

My girlfriend Dana told me she will never forget that day because she felt my pain. She said I was inside of a car balled up like a knot crying uncontrollably. Kiesha said I cried for days and days non-stop, I can still hear the sound of Kiesha's voice telling me, "It's going to be ok."

After Richard got killed, I stayed inside. There was no arrest made in his killing. Donnell was still missing. I went to work, came home, and stayed inside. My home was with Nia and Kiesha. Their mom let me stay with them. Mrs. Laura had a two bedroom apartment on 140th Street. Nia, Kiesha, Kimberly, Scottie, little Richard little Lamont, Mrs. Laura, myself and sometimes her man Ring Ding all stayed there. There was a lot of people staying at Mrs. Laura's house and I figured it would be good for Reshonia to stay with Velma. So Reshonia stayed with Velma.

About three weeks after Richard got killed, his little brother Donnell's body showed up. Donnell's body was discovered on a Sunday afternoon, January 28, 1990. His body was wrapped in plastic and discovered in Orchard Beach by a homeless man.

I was still mourning Richard when the kidnappers decided to throw

Donnell's body out in Orchard Beach, not too far from where Richard's body was left. I know Velma and Pat was hurt. Velma losing both of her sons and Pat losing both of her brothers I could have never imagined. The whole tragedy was real for them, and it was real for me that my daughter's father was gone. That was never the plan to take care of her on my own. But I have to say Richard warned me when he gave me the scenarios of the what ifs.

The day of Donnell's funeral I don't remember much but I do remember walking into Abyssinian Baptist Church on 138th in Harlem feeling empty. Even if I was with someone, I only remember being alone. I remember watching all of Donnell's little classmates from PS 192 crying and wiping their eyes. I remember hearing the chorus sing His Eye of the Sparrow by Lauryn Hill.

I never got a chance to really process Donnell dying.

Everything was happening so quick.

BACK OUTSIDE &
BROKEN

fter a few months of staying inside, I began to go back outside. One day, I was walking uptown, pushing Reshonia in her stroller. I was crossing 127th Street & 7th Ave. Alpo and some dude were on their motorcycles sitting at a red light. This was the very first time I had seen Alpo since Richard's death. I looked at Alpo and he looked at me. It was like we both said something to one another but we didn't. I could feel the energy, it was an energy of guilt and shame. I kept walking. Neither of us said a word, we just looked at each other.

Alpo and I were never the best of friends. I never really liked him. I'm sure he knew that I didn't care for him, but he didn't care.

Alpo used to fuck with me all the time. He would say shit like, "Ang, you number one or you number two?" That shit would get me heated and Alpo knew that. Even if I didn't care for Alpo, he would always have something to say. This day, he could not say anything. This is the man Richard asked to be Reshonia's godfather, and there I was with my daughter right in front of his face, and he didn't have a word to say.

In my mind, all I was saying was: Yeah, he did it. He killed Richard.

The next time I saw Alpo was a few months later at The Rink, in New Jersey. As soon as I saw him, my energy dropped. He was roller skating, and so was I, but once I recognized Alpo was there, there was no way we could be skating together. There was no way we could be partying together.

It was not officially confirmed that he killed Richard, and I don't even know if it was suspected—but I felt it in my heart.

I left the skate floor and sat down in the middle where there were seats. I watched him go around once. He saw me watching him, and next thing I knew he was leaving with his skates on his shoulders. My night was over after that. I put on my shoes and waited for my friends to be ready to leave.

My spirit did not sit well with Alpo. I didn't like his style and I never believed that he was a friend to Richard. It was just a few months before Richard got killed that I saw Alpo in the skating rink in New Jersey. It was around October, October 1989. My friends and I were leaving the skating rink, and he told some dude, "That's Rich baby mother but you can talk to her." I looked at Alpo and rolled my eyes. I never told Richard because I didn't want to start any trouble.

Today I feel much different, and I wish I would have told Richard what Alpo said. No, I don't take the blame and I'm not beating myself up but I will never hold back from telling my loved ones anything they need to know.

If I would have told Richard, maybe he would have had his guard up. Back then, I just didn't want to start any trouble. Richard loved Alpo and I really did not want to be the one to cause friction. Yes, I once told Richard I did not believe Alpo was his friend, but I never went into details. I told him Alpo was not his friend way before Alpo said what he said at The Rink. There's other reasons why I never told Richard what Alpo said besides not wanting to start trouble. I also didn't really know where I stood in Richard's life at the time. We had really just got back together. I knew Richard loved me, but I knew he loved Alpo, too. Regardless of how I felt then, I will never withhold information and not tell my loved ones when someone violates them.

I'm sure Richard was aware and watching out, especially with the circumstances at the time. He always told me when someone was not my friend. He would say, "Ang, you can't trust everyone. Everyone is not your friend." He would tell me to speak up when someone tries to hurt my feelings. "Say something back to hurt their feelings when they hurt your feelings. You can't be too nice, people will take advantage. " Richard didn't trust anyone either, but he trusted Alpo. Richard loved Alpo. Alpo is probably one of the only people who could have set Richard up the way he did. Because Richard really loved and trusted Alpo.

The weather started getting nice and I started going outside more and more. My friends all had children so we would meet up so they could play with each other. On the weekends I picked Reshonia up from Velma's. There was plenty of days Kiesha and I walked from 140th Street to St. Nick projects to see our friends. Kiesha would already have her son lil Richard and we always stopped on 132nd Street to pick up Reshonia from Velma's house. I'll never forget walking around 132nd and Johnny was there. It was a lot of people standing in front of Velma's building. Velma, Pat, Richard's Uncle Johnny aka Apple, his wife and his children.

Johnny's wife was pretty and was always very pleasant and polite. One would have never thought she would be involved with a man like

Johnny. Their sons were so sweet. I can still picture Johnny standing on the block of 132nd Street. I can still see his face, his smile, talking, and acting as if nothing happened. He would say, "Hey Reshonia." But for me, there was always something wicked about Johnny. He always gave me that drug addict desperate vibe. Whenever Johnny was there, I would get Reshonia and me out. I never really stayed around 132nd long anyway after Richard got killed. It was always crowded in front of Velma's building. Especially in the summertime everyone came by to show Velma and Pat love including all of Richard's girl friends that I knew nothing about when Richard was alive, but they made it their business to let me know the deal once Richard was dead. I truly didn't care.

Daniel, Richard's cousin, my foster sister Yvette's "husband" went to jail that summer, 1990, the summer right after Richard got killed. He got locked up for a case he caught in Virginia in the summer of 1989. According to public records he was convicted and sentenced to life. I never really knew his whole story because I was no longer living with Helen, Yvette, or Netta. In the 90's all the drug dealers were going to jail or getting killed; very few made it out with no bruises.

I started walking all over Harlem with Reshonia and my friends once Richard got killed. We walked up to Sugar Hill 145th and St. Nick, we walked up there to see the guys, we walked to Grant's Tomb with our strollers and kids. Whenever they were playing music we were there. I did exactly what Richard used to tell me not to do, I was walking the streets of Harlem every time the weather permitted.

That's when I fucked Azie. It was the beginning of the Summer of 1990, right after Richard got killed.

I can't remember where I was. I might have been walking, or maybe

I was standing on 140th Street; I don't remember. But I do remember Azie calling me over to his car. What kind of car? I can't remember, I just remember Azie calling me over to his car and asking me if I was okay. I said yes.

Azie asked me how Reshonia was doing. I told him she was okay. Azie took a stack of five dollar bills out of his pocket and handed it to me. "Take this for you and Reshonia."

I put the money in my pocket and thanked him. Azie told me to take his beeper number and beep him if I or Reshonia ever need anything.

As soon as Azie left, I went upstairs to see how much money he gave to me. He gave me five hundred dollars.

A few weeks went by and I decided to beep Azie and ask him for money to buy Reshonia a battery-operated Barbie car. I beeped Azie and he called me back. Azie asked me how much it cost. I told him it was two hundred and fifty dollars and he brought the money to me.

The first time I fucked Azie was at the music studio. He asked me to meet him on 142nd Street between Lenox and 5th Avenue, right by the Armory. Azie said he wanted me to hear some music he was working on and asked me if I would go to the studio with him. I said, Yes. I jumped in the car, and we drove off.

The music studio was downtown Brooklyn. A few of his friends were at the studio with us. I can't remember who all was there. I believe it was Diggaroo and Little Bop. They were Azie's friends. I believe they also rapped on his Mob Style album. Azie's record label was called Mob Style. The studio was a nice little hang out spot with chairs and a couch. It was really cozy with dim lights. We listened to some of the rap songs Azie and his friends recorded.

Azie and I talked about Richard for a little while. At that time, it was not confirmed that Alpo killed Richard.

We talked about the time he got robbed. The time when six people got shot up. Three died and three survived. Azie told me the whole story. Azie said he was coming from playing basket ball, he was with a 13 year old little girl, he didn't say that the girl was thirteen but the news reported that it was a 13 year old girl included in the shooting. Besides I knew the girl, she was about 4 or 5 years younger than me. Azie was 23 at the time, yeah a real creep. Azie said they was going to an apartment in the Bronx, it was him, the young girl, and a male friend of his. I forgot if Azie said if it was his apartment or not, but it obviously was where he stashed his money and drugs.

He said he knew something was not right when he got to the building because he asked Joanne or Myra to throw the keys out the window so he could get in the front door. He said the keys just came flying out the window. I believe Joanne and Myra lived in the apartment. Back then people use to let the drug dealers use their apartments and most of the time the drug dealers made sure the bills were paid. I did not know Joanne or Myra but my God mother Mrs.Laura was a bartender at the Third Palm bar uptown in Washington Heights. My God mother said they were partners and they both were very nice ladies. Azie said that the keys being thrown out the window was different because they never just threw the keys out the window like that. Azie said the three of them went upstairs and as soon as they got to the door, they were grabbed inside the apartment. Azie said Joanne and Myra was already tied up and on their knees waiting to be killed execution style. Azie said the killers took him straight into the bedroom to where the safe was. He said the killers kept asking him to open the safe and he refused. He heard gunshots in the other room. He said he knew one of the guys so he knew they were going to kill him anyway. Azie said after hearing the killers shoot everyone else, he began to fight for his life. While he was trying to fight the killers, they shot him multiple times. Then they left hoping that he was dead but he wasn't. I believe Azie said it was the young girl, Lynette, that crawled to the phone to call for help.

We talked, ordered food, and chilled for a little while, one thing led to the next and next thing I know Azie and I were having sex. I don't remember how it felt. I don't even remember where we had sex at or what was our sex position. I'm just guessing it was doggy style. I remember Azie saying he wanted to use my ass on his album cover. Azie said he liked the way my ass looked when he was fucking me. I did not plan on having sex with Azie. I just went along with the flow.

We had sex two other times and each time money was involved. I needed a few dollars so I beeped Azie. When Azie called me back, I told him I needed a few dollars. He said, ok and told me to meet him on 142nd Street where we met before. Right between Lenox and Fifth Avenue.

I met Azie and we went to a hotel in Jersey. I don't remember where the hotel was at in New Jersey or the name of the hotel. I just remember relaxing in the Jacuzzi waiting for Azie to come back from wherever he went. Azie dropped me off and said he had to make a run. When he came back, we ordered food, fucked and went to sleep. The next morning Azie gave me a thousand dollars and dropped me off in Harlem.

The last time Azie and I fucked, we were at his apartment in Parkchester. I had a beeper and Azie beeped me. I did not know it was Azie. I called the number back and Azie answered the phone. He said,

"Come to Parkchester. I got something for you. I'm going to send a cab to get you." Azie sent a cab to get me from 140th Street, and I went to Parkchester. Parkchester is a section of the Bronx. Azie had an apartment inside of Parkchester Condominium Complex.

When I got to Parkchester, Azie met me downstairs. The cab driver knew exactly where to go because he took me straight to where Azie was at.

The apartment was not furnished at all. I even believe there was a mattress on the floor. If I recall that's what we fucked on. Only this time it was no jacuzzi involved.

Clearly Azie called me up to Parkchester just to fuck. And that was ok with me because I never wanted a relationship with Azie. Azie was Richard's sister's child's father and he was supposed to be Richard's friend. I didn't want it to get out that I was fucking Azie. I was looking out for him like he was looking out for me until he got too comfortable with his hygiene situation. Like I said there was no jacuzzi and I guess before I got there Azie did not shower or take a bath because he was musky all over.

Afterwards he gave me a few dollars, five hundred dollars all single dollar bills to be exact. Azie called me a cab to go home, I went downstairs by myself got in the cab and I never fucked Azie again.

When Richard died, Azie was one of the only guys who asked me if Reshonia and I were ok. He asked me if a needed anything and gave me money. Oh my God he's so nice. He really cared about Richard I thought. I thought Azie was looking out for me because he was Richard's friend. But no, Azie was looking out for himself. He knew I was in need emotionally and financially. He took advantage of my vulnerability. I was twenty one, naïve and easy to deceive.

Azie wanted a taste of what Richard had. I remember the second time we had sex. Azie and I were at the hotel in New Jersey. Azie was fucking me from back and he said, "Now I know why Richard was so in love with you, this pussy is real good." I didn't say anything I never said much when I fucked back then I always stayed quiet even when I came.

I fell right into his trap.

After a while, I was outside and reckless. I was having sex with different guys, threesomes and a gang bang. That's the way I was coping with life. And that's another story to be told in another book.

There was a rumor in Harlem that I was sniffing cocaine but nah I never sniffed coke or did anything hard. I smoked a little marijuana now and then, but sex was my drug. I lost a lot of weight, I was already slim but I had gotten really skinny after Richard died, I probably didn't weigh no more than one hundred and twenty five pounds. That's probably why people may have thought I was using drugs.

It was the end of the summer 1990. I was still working at Interboro Institute but anytime a guy called me to go out of town I would leave work and go. It was like four different guys I was going out of town with around the same time. That shit was fun. Anytime they asked, I was ready to go. I would be at work and a guy would call and say, "Ang I'm going to western union you some money. I want you to come to DC, Baltimore and Virginia, whereever. " I would hang up the phone, wait a half a hour and tell my supervisor that I was sick. I would leave work, go to western union, and head to the airport or the Amtrak. I eventually got fired from my job because I was calling out to much. Guys used to pay me more than what I got paid so I chose to go out of town with them instead of going to work.

I never carried any drugs. I was way too scared to carry drugs but I did carry money back and forth. I was not thinking about the job security, the steady income, or the fact that what I was doing was money laundering. I was only thinking about having fun. In my mind I was saying he must like me because I'm carrying his money. Yeah stupid.

I got my own apartment fall of 1990, a female who lived in Nia and Kiesha's building asked me if I wanted her apartment because she was moving out. I said, Yes. I got my own apartment in the building. It was a one-bedroom apartment. Connie and I were still friends so she helped me fix it up. She gave me her living room set. She fixed up my bedroom with a queen-sized bed, two nightstands, a dresser, and she helped me dress the bed with a pretty comforter set. We went to Fordham Road up in the Bronx, and we got flowers, a vase, and a picture to decorate the place. It was nice and cute once Connie was finished.

I was so happy that I had a home that Reshonia could come to. I remember the day I was sitting on the couch watching Reshonia play. She was talking on her toy cell phone that Richard brought for her, "Daddy, daddy, can Shaquana come with us, ok daddy I love you." Reshonia was too young to know what happened to her father.

I was hanging out nonstop. I went roller skating at The Rink in New Jersey almost every Tuesday and Saturday. Fridays and Sundays were when most of the parties took place. The parties were at the Supper Club in Times Square, the Savoy Manor in the Bronx or the Cotton Club in Harlem. No matter where the party was—I was there.

In the early 1990's the parties were popping. Music artists, athletes, hustlers, and the general population all partied together.

Hip Hop started emerging in the mid 80's and most of the rappers came from the black communities, communities of poverty, filled with substance use, drug dealers and lots of crime. Rap was created through these circumstances, and it was the way some of those affected expressed themselves.

A lot of the rappers and drug dealers worked together to change the game and they played together to celebrate the gains. Some rappers used the profit from selling drugs to support their rap career. Then there were some drug dealers that saw rappers as another product to pimp. Either way when it came to partying in my day, we all partied together. Plenty of athletes were inspired by drug dealers and rappers. It was the lifestyle. The money, the fame, the cars, the trips, the females, and they would be at all the parties.

It was nothing to go to the club and see a hip hop artist or an athlete on the dance floor dancing right next to you. I've been in the club with Biggie, Treach, Big L, Herb Mcgruff, Monifa, Allen Iverson, Mike Tyson, Diddy, Camron, Mase, Foxy Brown, Little Kim, Eve, and so many others.

I remember being in a club, I forget which one maybe the Tunnel or the Supper Club, I'm not sure but I remember going to the ladies room and Mary J Blige was in the ladies room. She said, "I like your shoes." I was like wait a minute was that Mary J Blige? And did she tell me she liked my shoes? Yes, it was Mary J Blige and she was just that cool.

The Best Out gave some of the best parties at the Cotton Club. There were a few groups of guys in Harlem that promoted parties and the Best Out was one of theirs. The Best Out, The Same Gang, and The Final Four. Those three were the only groups I knew of back then. There may have been more groups, I'm not sure, but I believe those were the top three. The Best Out always gave the best parties, in my opinion. Damon Dash was like one of the CEO's of the Best Out.

Most of the Best Out parties took place at the Cotton Club on 125th Street on Broadway in Harlem. When the Best Out gave a party people came from all over. I'm not sure about the females, but I know the guys were coming from Harlem, The Bronx, Brooklyn, Queens and Staten Island. Guys were even coming from Newark, East Orange, and Patterson New Jersey, for The Best Out parties.

I knew Damon before I had Reshonia. I met Damon through the guys from my block, 142nd Street. Damon went to Manhattan Center High School and played basketball with a few of them. I'm not sure if they played on a team together or just for fun but I know they played basketball ball together. I was about 15 or 16 years old. I was always cool with most of the guys from the block. We were all like family. Sometimes Damon and the guys would come to my high school, Julia Richmond on 68th to pick up some of their friends that lived on 142nd Street. We all took the train or the bus uptown together. I remember one day we were coming from school. It was a few of us on the train going home. I was with my girls and Damon was with his guy friends. We were all friends. I remember getting into a debate with Damon and his friends about who is better, Black girls or Puerto Rican girls. Damon and a few of his friends were saying that Puerto Rican girls were better because they have better hair, and they talk that Spanish shit in your ear. Me and my girlfriends cursed Damon and his friends out. Now when I see his choice in women I'm never surprised

Damon also hung out in my foster mother Helen's house. Helen's house was the "hang out" house. Damon used to come up to my foster mother's apartment a lot to hang out even after I had Reshonia.

All the guys knew Reshonia was Richard's daughter, so they always gave her a lot of attention, well I should say they always acknowledged her. Whenever Richard came to the block to pick up Reshonia, myself or the both of us, all the guys in the block would just stand on the corner watching.

I remember one New Years Eve the whole block was at Helen's house including Damon, we brought in the New Years together. Damon and I were not the best of friends, but we were ok.

About ten months after Richard got killed, Damon and I messed around. It wasn't anything serious, it was just something that happened. My friend Shia and I went out to eat with Damon and his friend Eric. Back then guys always invited females out to eat. It didn't have to mean that you were in a relationship with the dude. Damon already knew I was staying on 140th Street. When you're from the hood everybody knows where everybody lives. That's just how it is. Damon and Eric came and picked us up in a cab from 140th Street and we went to Land and Sea, a restaurant in the Bronx off of Broadway. Back then I did not smoke weed, but I did drink and so did Damon. As a matter of fact, I recall seeing Damon pissy drunk at a couple of parties. I drank a lot too back then but thank God I knew how to hold my composure. At least until I got behind closed doors because that's when I became a freak. Lord knows whenever I had a few too many drinks my legs were ready to open wide. And that's exactly what happened this night. We all got tipsy and Damon and I decided to take a cab to a hotel in the Bronx. I don't remember what hotel, but I do remember it was right off a highway. Shia and Eric got in the cab and went home.

When we got to the hotel, both of us immediately took our clothes off. Damon was drunk and so was I. I was hot, horny and ready for him to put it in. I felt his penis. It was hard and so big. I was kind of scared. I got in the shower and when I got out, he got in the shower. We didn't take a shower together because this was not a love thing, it was just a fuck. I lay in the bed waiting with my fingers in my wet wet vagina. Damon got out of the shower, came in the room, got in the bed and immediately got on top of me. He wasted no time putting his big penis in me. Thank God I'm blessed to have a wet vagina because, if not, I would have been completely raw. As soon as Damon put his penis in my vagina he went to town.

He was fucking me like he was having a seizure and he came so fast that he apologized immediately after, "I'm sorry, I was so excited."

"If you would have slowed down, maybe you would not have cum so fast. Get up off of me, please," I said. I showered, and when Damon went to the shower, I took whatever cash he had in his pockets. I'm not even that type of chick and was never that type of chick but something had to give. I waited for Damon to get out of the shower. When Damon got out of the shower, he called a cab. When the cab came, we both got in and Damon dropped me off at my apartment building on 140th Street. He apologized for his wack ass sex the whole way there. I don't even know if he realized I took some of his money. It was not much and it damn sure wasn't worth it.

The next day, Damon came to my apartment on 140th Street. He just popped up at my apartment door, unexpectedly. I did not know he was coming but I still let him in. Reshonia was at Velma's house, and I was home by myself.

As soon as I let Damon in my apartment he said, "Let me get another chance."

"Nah, no second chances," I said.

We were in the hallway right by the door. My bedroom was to the right. He was persistent and kept trying to push himself on. I kept backing up until I was in my bedroom. I fell back on the bed and Damon started to get on top of me. That's when I lied and said, "I have herpes." He was becoming persistent and forceful but when I said I had herpes, he left me alone. That was the last time Damon ever tried to have sex with me.

I went to a lot of events. One event I went to but did not go into was the charity basketball ball game that Puffy gave at City College. I wanted to go and I went to the college but it was way too crowded. And it just seemed like too much going on. One thing about me I like to go out, but I don't believe in waiting in no line, I will leave right away and that's what I did. I'm glad because that night it was a massacre.

In 1991 Alpo was arrested in the state of Maryland and was convicted on 13 counts of murder including Richard Porter. Alpo snitched on a lot of people and instead of a death sentence, he was sentenced 25 to life.

According to the story Alpo gave to Troy Reed on a YouTube video he killed Richard that night. The night of January 3rd 1990. Alpo said he picked Richard up in Harlem. I'm not sure where he picked Richard up but I'm sure it was somewhere around 124th Street on the west side of Harlem. I'm guessing somewhere around 124th Street because he said he gave the dude Big Head Gary from DC the sign to kill Richard not too long after Richard got into the van. Alpo said he killed Richard right in front of what is now the Harlem Shake, a burger joint located at 100 West 124th Street. That's on 124th Sstreet in Harlem right between Adam Clayton Powell and Lenox Avenue, actually it's right on the corner of

124th and Lenox Avenue. Back in 1990 I'm sure it was nothing more than an abandoned building and I'm pretty sure no one around. I may not be right about everything but I know Richard was under pressure when he called me. I don't know if Richard was already in the van with Alpo when he called me or if he was waiting for Alpo to pick him up.

Alpo said in one of his YouTube videos that he got his money back from Richard because he took what Richard had that night. In my opinion he just wanted a reason to rob Richard, his greed out of control. Everybody he killed he said he took something from them. Money or drugs. I listened to a few of the YouTube videos with Alpo explaining why he killed Richard. I listen to them because I'm always hoping to hear some type of remorse but instead he showed no remorse at all. In my opinion he seems to think that killing Richard was a joke and he shows no sympathy for any of the families of those he killed.

I dealt with different guys from 1990 until 1994 until I met my youngest daughter's father around March of 1994. I met my youngest daughter's father outside of the club. My energy was always upbeat when I was out, guys always brought me drinks and when they did buy me a drink, I never allowed them to stay in my space. I always wanted to bounce around the club and have fun. I loved to dance nasty and when I rubbed my ass against a niggar, I often made myself cum. I had fun when I went out.   One night I was coming from a club in Harlem. The club was near 125th Street right off 12th Avenue. Back then the clubs on 12th Avenue in Harlem looked like warehouses. I came out the door, there was several niggars trying to talk to me, I remember brushing them off, and making my way out of the door.   I got out the door and stood across the street waiting for all my friends. This dude was sitting in the front seat of a SUV and he said, "My man wanna talk to you." I said,

"Your man don't have a mouth of his own?" My daughter's father was sitting in the back seat. I looked in the car window and he asked me for my number. I gave him my number, but I was not interested. The fact that he was in the back seat and another niggar had to speak for him just turned me off. I gave him my number and every time he called me, I was unavailable. I remember one time I picked up the phone and told him I had company.

A few weeks later I saw my daughter's father inside of The Rink in New Jersey. It was a Saturday night. The rink was really crowded. So crowded they didn't even have skates for rent. It was a Saturday night so it made sense but I recall it was Easter Sunday weekend. I was sitting down when he said hi and asked me why wasn't I skating. "They don't have any skates my size, they're all sold out." He left me sitting there and came back with a brand new pair of skates for me. I was impressed not because he purchased the skates for me but because once he gave me the skates, he left the skating rink. That was all part of the game.

After that day we dated all the time, every day he came to pick me up from work, we went bowling and shot pool together. He took me to Miami for the 4th of July that year and by then I was already pregnant. To make a long story short I didn't really know him and he didn't really know me.

I ended up moving to Georgia at the end of the summer in 1996, after my daughter's father hit me in my head so hard with my shoe that I had two black eyes for about two months. I still have a knot on my head today. When he hit me, I knew I had to do something because my daughters were watching. My daughters could see that my eyes were black.

Reshonia was eight years old and very much aware of what was going on. I knew I could not let her see that he hit me, and I did nothing about it. I had to make a serious move for myself and my daughters. When he hit me, it was late at night so I did not leave that night but the next morning I took my daughters and left. I left my apartment on 113th Street and St. Nicholas Avenue, left all of my furniture and most of my clothes. I left my job. My daughters and I got on the bus at the Port Authority and we went to Georgia.

I chose to go to Georgia because I knew my sister Leah was there. I wanted to be with my biological sister. My sister had just got out of prison about two years before and she decided to move to Georgia. We stayed with my sister, her husband, and her little son. That did not work out. My sister and I did not get along. Her son and my younger daughter did not get along. They were both babies. My younger daughter was about 18 months and my sister's son was 2 and some months. They used to fight a lot and my sister and I used to argue a lot. I did not have a car, so I worked up the road at a restaurant as a waitress. I was trying to save money to get my own apartment, but it was hard. I had to give my sister money for bills, and I had to feed my two daughters. I was not making a lot of money at the restaurant so saving up seemed impossible. I didn't have a car, so my job opportunities were limited and most opportunities were below my skill set. I was depressed, I was crying everyday. I became hopeless and I felt like I needed my daughter's father. I ended up going right back to my younger daughter's father.

My daughter's father did not know where I was because I never told him that I was leaving. I just up and left. I hadn't contacted him for two months or more. I wrote him a letter. I forget everything thing I wrote but I do remember feeling like he was the only person I had to help me.

I asked my daughter's father to send me money. He sent me money and then he came to Georgia to give me a used car that he brought for me. I was able to get a better job and my own apartment in Georgia. My daughter's father continued to live in New York, which was ok with me.

We didn't have a good relationship before he hit me in my head. We were not a match. I was too young to understand that. I was 25 years old when I met my youngest daughter's father. He seemed to be nice. I took him for face value without ever getting to know him. I guess it wasn't that I was too young, I didn't realize that it takes time to get to know a person.

After I moved to Georgia in the winter of 1996, I heard that Richard's uncle Johnny got arrested and was associated in the kidnapping of Richard's little brother Donnell, his own nephew. According to the news, Johnny was associated with a guy named Preacher. I had heard of Preacher and his crew, and I may have seen him once or twice but I didn't know him. I heard that he was extorting Richard when Richard was alive, but I never asked Richard, I would have never hurt Richard's pride like that.

Preacher and his crew were known for doing notorious crimes in Harlem since1983. The name of his crew was The Preacher Crew, and they did kidnappings, murders, rape, extorted drug dealers and robbed them. In February 1999 Preacher pleaded guilty to 13 counts of murder including Richard's little brother in order to avoid the death penalty. As for Johnny, I'm really not sure if Johnny was ever charged with kidnapping Donnell but I know for sure they all were nothing but monsters. Years later I found out that Preacher was also involved in kidnapping Bobby Brown and demanded money from Whitney.

I was glad I moved to Georgia around that time because there was a lot going on in Harlem. You really didn't know who was who. You didn't know who to trust.

Opportunity
to Exploit

⁓⫯⁓

I was living in Georgia when a few projects that included Richard's story were being put together, including the FEDs magazine and the Paid in Full movie that was being made primarily by Damon Dash.

When the first issue of the magazine came out, the FEDS magazine CEO said that Alpo admitted to killing Richard in an interview.

My younger daughter's father never once told me anything about this magazine. I found out about the magazine because my friend Claudia from Harlem mailed a copy of the magazine to me. I didn't know she was mailing it to me, she just mailed it. One day I received a yellow envelope in the mail and the magazine was inside. I can't remember what year it was and I don't remember what issue she sent to me but I do remember seeing Alpo's face on the cover. I believe it was 1997 or 1998. When Claudia sent the magazine I immediately called her up to ask about the cover of the magazine which was a picture with a group of guys from Harlem including Richard and Alpo. She told me that my daughter's father was a part of the magazine. I looked inside of the magazine at the section where the titles and credits were listed, and I saw his name. I forget what his title was, but I know his name was listed in the magazine.

I asked my daughter's father about the magazine. I asked him if it was legal for them to include Richard in the magazine without consent. I asked was it legal for them to profit with a murderer telling his own story. I don't remember exactly what his answer was, but I'm sure it was not helpful. I really had no knowledge about intellectual property rights but it didn't seem right.

I did my own research to see if it was legal and I was told that the magazine's distribution amount at the time was not enough to do anything about it. Honestly, from what I know now I don't think I would have been able to do anything about the magazine anyway.

I moved back to New York in 2000, when the Paid in Full movie was in production. I saw Damon, when the Willy Burger scene in the Paid in Full movie was being shot in Harlem on 145th between 7th and 8th Avenue.

Damon's team wanted me to give consent for Reshonia to be an extra. I refused to sign because my child was not an extra. Richard was my daughter's father. Besides, I had never seen a manuscript or anything. I did not know what the movie was about and how it was going to portray my daughter's father. I cared about Richard, and I care about how he is portrayed. Now Damon may have felt like that was a way for Reshonia to benefit but I saw things differently.

I don't really remember how I received the consent, but I did have a conversation with Pat, Richard's sister, about the Paid in Full project. Honestly, I forget if it was in person or if it was over the phone when I spoke to Pat about the movie. I asked Pat who gave Azie or Damon

Dash the rights to portray Richard in the Paid in Full movie. Her exact words were "This is A's story, this is not about Richard." Let's keep it real, there would be no Paid in Full story without Richard's story.

I'm glad I never signed any agreement with the Paid in Full movie.

I had a lawyer write a letter to Damon Dash, Miramax Films, Dimension Films and any other entity that was related. The letter asked for a college scholarship for Reshonia. When Reshonia graduated from high school, she went to Hofstra University, on Long Island. After two semesters, she had to come home because I could not afford for her to stay at Hofstra.

Damon's lawyer sent a letter back saying that Richard never knew his daughter. I don't know why they assumed that Richard did not know his daughter. I know Damon knew that Richard knew his daughter. I'm sure Damon witnessed Richard coming to see his daughter plenty of times. Damon did not know Richard, he knew me. Damon was a fan of Richard. He was one of the guys standing on the sidewalk every time Richard came to see me just admiring everything about Richard. And I'm almost 100% sure Richard didn't know Damon, not even his name.

It would really be hard for me to believe that Damon truly thought that Richard did not know his daughter. Now what Damon may have been led to believe is that my daughter didn't have Richard's name on her birth certificate. However, my daughter is the only person with Richard Shelton Porter's name and signature on her birth certificate.

Damon's lawyer said they did not need any consent and Reshonia was never included in the conversation anyway. I felt so disrespected, not only for myself, but also for Richard. As soon as I read the letter, I felt like I didn't matter. Completely ignored and not acknowledged at all.

Reshonia, myself, or Richard. I could never see a family member or a friend die or get killed and not look out for the child if I was in a position to do so. I didn't know that people were so wicked when it came to money. I don't even know what I did with the letters. However, if needed, I should be able to get the letters because everything was sent through their registered agent. The letter did not say anything threatening, and I didn't asked for a million dollars. We asked for a college scholarship.

One day I saw him on 20th Street at an Indian Restaurant. He was with his wife, Rachel Roy, the mother of his daughters. He said, "Hi Ang. You still have a cute face." I said, "Thank you." He asked me what did I think about the Paid in Full movie. He was excited and gave me the impression that he thought I would be excited too. I had not seen the movie and I damn sure was not excited. I felt more disrespected than anything. I let Damon know how I felt then. I don't remember exactly what I said but he got the message. Damon asked me, "What can you do Ang?" Before I could answer he said, "Give me your number." I wrote my number down and gave it to him. He went inside the restaurant with his wife and daughters. Damon never called me. When Damon asked me what could I do, I took it as if he was saying, I might have an opportunity for you, what can you do. But he never called me, so I really don't know what he was trying to say.

A few years later, I saw Damon on 14th Street between 7th and 8th Avenue. He was standing in front of a brownstone, 241 West 14th Street to be exact. My coworker and I were heading home from work. I worked in the Port Authority building which is now the Google building. One Eleven 8th Avenue between 15th and 16th Street. I can't remember what year it was when I saw Damon. I know it was somewhere around 2008. I remember the weather being nice and I believe it was spring time.

Damon was standing in front of a brownstone with a bunch of guys including Jim Jones.

There was some type of event going on because there were people dressed up standing on the stairs of the brownstone and I could see through the window that there was a lot going on inside.

Damon and I both noticed each other at the same time. He saw me walking down the block and I saw him standing there in front of the brownstone. We greeted each other with a smile, a hello and a hug.

All of that was good and I appreciated the love, but I still needed to speak my mind regarding his response to the letter that my lawyer sent him. I told my coworker she could go ahead because I needed to talk to Damon for a minute. My coworker kept walking and I stayed there with Damon.

The first thing I asked Damon was why didn't he look out for Richard's daughter. All I asked for was a scholarship. Damon said Richard's sister said she was going to look out. I said, "But Damon, you knew me, you didn't know Richard or his sister." Damon started to get loud and began to criticize my communication skills. I forgot exactly what he said but I believe he said something about my speech.

Damon's entourage came rushing over. Jim Jones stopped them before they could say anything to me. Jim Jones said, "Let her speak her peace." Damon's entourage backed off and went back to their standing position.

I had never met Jim Jones before but I knew that was Jim. That was really nice, I appreciated him for taking up for me.

I ignored Damon trying to belittle me and continued to express how

I felt about the Paid in Full project.

"How would you feel if you got killed and someone made a movie portraying you? A movie showing you getting shot down on the big screen—and no compensation was given to your children out of compassion. How would you feel if someone benefited off of your death and never contributed positively to your child's misfortune?" I asked.

Reshonia was 14 years old when Paid in Full was released. She was not a little baby. I was surprised that someone could make a fortune off of a deceased person without acknowledging the misfortune.

Damon started to say something about people uptown but I cut him off.

I said, "I'm not people from uptown. I live up the block."

I pointed my finger towards 7th Avenue.

"I'm all right, I live in a luxury building and my children are "A" students. I didn't ask you for anything for myself, I asked you for a scholarship for college for Richard's daughter."

Before I walked off, I said, "The right thing would have been for you to look out for Richard's child. The children are the future, Damon. Reshonia is a good girl with a lot of potential. If you are going to give, you should give the hand that's going to keep giving. Nothing ever lasts when you don't do shit right." I walked away and that was the last time I saw Damon.

I never cared for Damon's character, he always came off as arrogant and seemed to have a narcissistic personality to me. When it comes to him and Jay Z breaking up, I'm not surprised. Damon was an asshole when it came to Jay Z. I witnessed him trying to play Jay Z one day.

He was trying to make fun of Jay Z looks. Damon and Jay Z were in the bodega on 139th Street in Harlem. Right on 7th Avenue on the southeast corner. As soon as I walked into the Bodega, Dame said, "Ang would you talk to this nigger." I didn't know who Jay Z was at the time, but I knew he was not from Harlem. I could tell by the way he was dressed. I could tell he was from Brooklyn. I believe he had on a jean suit. Whatever it was it looked weird to me. Brooklyn guys always dressed weird to me. I was never a fan of Brooklyn guys because they never knew how to say hi without pulling my arm or some dumb shit.

When Damon asked me if I would talk to Jay Z, I told him to stop playing with me. I didn't appreciate the fact that he was trying use me to make a joke out of Jay Z.

This happened around the mid 90's. I don't believe Roc-a Fella was established yet. Anyway the way I see it, Damon didn't understand blessings versus luck. Damon was lucky to have Jay Z. Jay Z is blessed with a gift from God. Which is his talent. Damon was lucky to have a Jay Z. Luck runs out, blessings keep coming.

I'm glad I never signed any agreement with the Paid in Full movie because I disagree with the way Richard was portrayed. Mekhi Phifer did an excellent job. But the narrative was off. I didn't like that the movie was trying to make its audience believe that all Richard cared about was selling drugs and getting money. Richard had a vision and his determination to level up confused most that did not understand his attitude towards life. Even those that were supposed to be his family misunderstood his determination, his confidence, his pride and drive to level up.

In the state of New York, deceased individuals do not have publicity rights after death, but damn, I would think, giving the child something would be a moral obligation. However, clearly, everyone's morals and values are different.

I've always wondered if our sexual experience had anything to do with him not looking out for Reshonia when he made the Paid in Full film.

In May of 2007, Azie lied and said I cut him. If he was Richard's friend, why would he accuse Richard's daughter's mother of cutting him? Azie knew I did not cut him.

When Azie wrote the book, Game Over: The Rise and Transformation of a Hustler, he told me that Simon Schuster the book publishing company asked him to get consent to use Richard's name in his book. That meant that Azie needed to contact the next of kin to Richard. Which is my daughter, Reshonia. Reshonia is next of kin and she is the Administrator of Richard's Estate.

Azie didn't really need consent because deceased people don't have publicity rights after death in the state of New York. However, Simon and Schuster, the book publishers, must have thought it would be a good idea to get consent anyway. I believe it was sometime in 2006 that Azie contacted me about getting consent.

Azie contacted me and we arranged a date and time for him to drop the manuscript off so I could read it. When Azie dropped the manuscript off, he said something about giving me ten thousand dollars. I did not give a fuck about ten thousand dollars. That was no money to me. I agreed to meet with him because I really wanted the opportunity to tell him how I felt about the Paid in Full project. We met at my apartment, and I admit that was dumb. Because you never give up your address, but I was not thinking and I was thirsty to express myself. Not that it mattered but I just needed to be heard.

I had already spoken to Richard's sister Pat over the phone about how I felt about the Paid in Full project   I asked her how could she leave Richard's daughter out of the agreement. Pat said, "We didn't know what we were signing." That was the end of the conversation; I had nothing else to say to Pat.

When Azie came to my apartment, I told him how I felt. Reshonia and a couple of her guy friends were visiting on the same day Azie came. I expressed to Azie how I felt about no one looking out for Richard's daughter. I let Azie know that I felt it was very disrespectful to me and Richard. Reshonia asked Azie if he was her father's friend, why didn't he make sure she was included in the agreement. Azie didn't know what to say. At one point he was like, "Damn I feel Rich spirit in here." I guess he was feeling a little pressured, especially when Reshonia asked him why didn't look out for her.

Azie said that Damon did him dirty and that Damon only gave him $50,000. I said $50,000 and he basically said in so many words he didn't know what he was signing off on.

I didn't even read the whole manuscript because after a few pages I noticed how Azie was trying to downplay Richard. Trying to make Richard out to be some grimy guy. In the manuscript, Azie said Richard came to him and told him he had two babies on the way at the same time and he felt bad for killing someone. I forget exactly what it said but I do know he was trying to downplay Richard. Richard did not have two babies on the way at the same time. Richard was never convicted of shooting or killing anyone. Even if Richard was supposed to have killed someone, he was not here to defend himself. I was not going to just agree with what someone else said about him. Richard killing someone was not public record. He was never convicted of killing anyone. If he did kill someone, he never shared that information with me.

I was also tired of all the low-quality projects Azie and others were creating. None of the stories really represented Richard for who he really was. In the Paid in Full movie, it portrayed Richard as Mitch, a drug dealer still living at home with his mother and only caring about material things and fame. That was not Richard.

Richard was all about the hustle. The hustling game gave him the opportunities to move his family forward. It wasn't about the fans, Richard always showed love to all that showed love to themselves. But selling drugs and risking his life for fame or the fans, in my opinion was downplaying Richard's character.

So, I never signed any document giving my consent. I definitely was not signing off on something that I did not agree with for ten thousand dollars.

One day Azie put something on MySpace that bothered Reshonia. Reshonia called me, upset. Reshonia said Azie posted somewhere on social media that he was Richard's friend before she was Richard's daughter. I don't know what he meant when he said that but it was real ignorant of him to say that. It made Reshonia cry, and I was hurt.

When I got off the phone, I told my younger daughter's father, they're only taking advantage because they know I don't have anyone. A lot of people in Harlem knew I did not have a lot of family. A lot of guys knew I didn't have the information, support, or money to stop them from using Richard to profit. My youngest daughter's father would be around some of these people sometimes. In my mind, I was like Why don't you ask them why don't they look out for Richard's daughter?

Every invention has a social effect. Reshonia was almost fifteen years old when the Paid in Full movie came out. Regardless of how many people liked her father there are just as many people who liked Alpo. No one ever thought about the bullying or negative remarks she might have had to endure or the emotional effects she would experience from that movie.

The FEDS told me that anything Richard had belonged to Reshonia and because she was a minor that would mean it would go to me. Maybe that's Damon and his friends didn't acknowledge Reshonia, because they didn't want to acknowledge me. I don't know and I don't care, it was completely immoral. Rich knew I was a survivor and he knew if something ever happened to him, his child was going to be alright.

One evening, when the restaurant closed, I, my youngest daughter, and a little girl named Shannon that I used to watch got in my daughter father's car. My daughter's father always drove us home after the restaurant closed, whenever I helped him out there. We got into the car and drove off. Only this night my daughter's father decided to drive up to 146th Street and St. Nicholas Avenue. Azie's mother lived there, and Azie hung out in front of the building. I didn't know my daughter's father was going to drive there. When I realized where he was going, I thought maybe he is going to say something to Azie about fucking with my child.

We pulled up to 146th Street and St. Nicholas Avenue—right in front of Azie's mother's building. My daughter's father and I both got out of the car. My younger daughter and the little girl Shannon stayed in the car. My daughter was twelve and Shannon was four years old.

I don't remember exactly what I said to Azie when I got out of the car. My daughter's father reached Azie first. I was walking towards Azie, and I was upset, screaming, "Why are you fucking with my daughter?" I said it a few times as I walked toward Azie. Before I could get close to Azie to talk to him, I noticed he was holding the top of his head with his right hand. I saw my daughter's father running back to the car, so I ran back to the car too. I did not know what was going on. Everything happened so fast. I never got the chance to talk to Azie about upsetting Reshonia.

My daughter's father dropped off Shannon and then he dropped me and my little daughter off at my building on West 15th Street. My daughter's father left, we were not together and he was not allowed to stay at my apartment.

As soon as I got upstairs Pat called me cursing me out calling me all types of names. I told her I didn't cut Azie and I may have said something about Reshonia being Richard's daughter. I'm not sure but I clearly remember her saying, "Before he had a daughter, he had a mother." I thought his mother was responsible for him and Richard was responsible for his daughter. So respectfully, if you're going to use his legacy for proceeds, at least contribute to some of his daughter's needs. Any way some people will never get it, and I get it. After I got off the phone, I took a bath and went to sleep.

Bang Bang Bang! It was five o'clock the next morning when two police officers came banging on my door. They were dressed in regular clothes. Only myself and my younger daughter were at home.

I opened the door and they basically bust in. I picked up the phone and called the police on them. My younger daughter woke up and started to cry. The police from my community downtown came to my apartment, they were regular uniformed police men and were unable to do anything. The regular dressed police explained that they were from the 30th precinct and said some other stuff to them. I don't remember what they said but I do remember the police in uniform could do nothing to help me.

They asked me if I cut Azie. I told them I did not cut Azie.

"Well why would he say you cut him if you did not cut him?"

I told the police I did not know what Azie was talking about.

I had a tee shirt and panties on. The tee shirt had a picture of Richard on the front. The police officers told me to get dressed because they were taking me to the precinct. I went in my room and closed the door behind me. One of the officer's kicked the door open. I did not know that I was not supposed to close the door.

My younger daughter was crying, out of control. The police officers asked me if I had someone to come take care of my daughter. I called a friend who lived nearby and she said she was coming. I talked to my younger daughter and tried to calm her down. I told her I would be okay and that my friend Matty was coming to get her.

After I talked to my daughter, the police handcuffed me. My daughter stood at the door, crying. The police took me downstairs. I was so embarrassed. My concierge and building porter watched as the police escorted me out of the building. We walked to a dark-colored van and the police opened the door and I got in. During the ride to the precinct, I did not say a word. Once we got to the precinct, they kept asking me about cutting Azie. I told them over and over again that I did not cut him.

I could not believe I was being arrested for something I did not do.

The police officer checked my records. "Damn, girl, you got a clean record."

I said, "Yes, that's why I don't understand why you are arresting me because a drug dealer lied about me."

In the back of my mind, I was talking to God. God why did this happen. Did my daughter's father cut Azie? I didn't actually see him cut Azie so I could not say that he did. I questioned myself about whether I provoked or agitated the situation.

The officers kept asking me questions. I refused to answer any questions, but I let the officers know over and over again I did not cut Azie.

I stayed at the precinct all day. That evening, they said they had to take me down to central booking to go to court so they took me downtown.

I was thinking it was a good thing. I was glad the police were finally taking me downtown to see the judge. In my mind, once I saw the judge, I would be able to go home. I did not cut Azie and I've never done anything wrong. Why would the judge not let me go home?

Well, I was completely wrong because the judge did not let me go. The district attorney presented the case to the judge. The DA said that I cut Azie over royalties for the Paid in Full film. I was like, "What the fuck is he talking about?" At that time, I didn't know about anyone getting royalties.

It was terrible. My little daughter was sitting in the court room by herself. I was so hurt when I looked out and saw her sitting on the bench by herself. I thought, Why the fuck would her father send her in the courtroom by herself? And it was night court which made it even worse. I was livid that she had to see the court officers take me back to the cell so I could go to Rikers. I was so worried about her. And if he cut Azie and he cared anything about me, he would have never allowed me to take the blame.

Today, I believe that some of Richard's family received royalties from the Paid In Full movie. If I'm not mistaken, they receive royalties from being an extra. To be fair, I refused to sign the consent for Reshonia because I didn't know enough about the project. I really can't be mad about the royalties and I'm not. Damon is always calling someone a culture vulture. He even wrote a book about culture vultures which I'm sure it was easy to write because he is a culture vulture himself.

The DA spoke to the judge. Afterwards, the judge made his decision. His decision was to hold me and he set bail. I never got a chance to talk but I was able to plead not guilty. I believe the bail was six thousand dollars. I did not have six thousand dollars. I had to go to Rikers Island. On the way to Rikers, there were other people on the bus. A young man noticed my tee shirt and said he was from Harlem. He said he heard of Richard Porter. I can't remember the young man's first name, but I do know his last name was Frost.

The bus stopped at the female facility, and I got off. Before I got off the bus, I told the young man to be careful and be safe. I never saw him again.

I wasn't really scared when I was locked up, but I definitely felt violated. I had to take off all of my clothes in front of female guards. Every now and then a guard would say, "Oh you new. This must be your first time." There were beautiful young girls strung out on dope in prison for shoplifting. That was a sight to see. It really made me think about my daughters and thank God that they are not on drugs. Rikers was really no fun. When you go to Rikers, you have to take an AIDS test. You have to see the doctor and they take a few tests. They ask you if you want the results told to you or mailed to your home. I was like mail the results to my house. I did not know my status at the time because I had not taken a test since I last fucked and I definitely was not trying to find out if I was negative or positive while I was in jail.

God had to sit me down, put me on time out, time to myself, and time to think. How the hell did I get here I asked myself? Before this incident I spent days researching, writing letters to different people asking about publicity rights. I even wrote a letter in support of the Marilyn Monroe publicity rights legislation. I received a letter back saying that my story was compelling. I emailed everyone I thought was connected to the Paid in Full movie. I tried to contact the Shawn Carter scholarship program to ask for a scholarship for Reshonia. I emailed Beyoncé and I pray she did not get it because I said some not so nice words. I was a mess, depressed, crying everyday, and not present. It had to happen. I needed to realize that I needed to let go and let God.

I didn't eat the whole time I was on Rikers Island. I drank a cup of milk because the correctional officer told me to, but other than that, I had nothing in my stomach. At one point, I started to cry and one of the CO's told me not to do that. I wiped my eyes immediately. After the CO told me not to cry, I fixed my composure and sat up straight. She was right I needed to stay strong, and crying is a sign of weakness in jail. I definitely didn't need to let the other inmates see me as a weak link.

After 3 days of being locked up on Rikers Island, my daughter's father bailed me out.

I was scared to death when I had to go to court. My court date was in August of 2007. About two months after the incident. I didn't realize I was so scared until the court date. My heart was racing, and I felt like I was having an anxiety attack; the thought of going back to Rikers Island was traumatizing.

I could not afford a lawyer, so I had a legal aide representing me. When my case was called, the judge saw that Azie did not show up in court and the case was dismissed. I have not seen or heard anything about Azie since then. Well I have seen him on different YouTube videos every now and then but I don't make it a habit of watching what's not good for my soul.

I got a lawyer to get the case expunged and he also assisted with Reshonia becoming the Administrator of Richard's estate. Richard's mother, Velma, helped to make Reshonia Administrator of Richard's estate by signing the necessary documents before she died in 2012.

Velma loved Reshonia and she knew how much Richard loved his daughter.

Velma was around to see Richard's love for me. Pat was never around to see Richard's love for his daughter or for me.

Velma called me up one day after she signed the documents and asked me if I had any money. I told her yes, so we agreed to meet at the 135th Street train station on Lenox Avenue. I really didn't like being in Harlem after Azie accused me of cutting him, so I wanted to meet Velma and get right back on the train.

When we met at the train station, Velma said, "I know you didn't cut that mother fucker. Pat is letting Azie run all over me. I can't stand that mother fucker, him or Damon Dash. I'm going to write my own book,

I got something for these mother fuckers." Velma said she was working on her own book about her life story.

Velma said that people in Harlem believed that I was having a nervous breakdown. Because that's what my daughter's father was going around saying.

I was having a lot of challenges but thank God I never had a nervous breakdown.

Being locked up gave me a lot of time to think. What could I have done different? I thought about the phrase "Let go and let God." That's what I needed to do. I needed to let go and let God. I was doing too much. I was stressing myself out and I was stressing my children out. I was trying to fix what I believe was wrong on my own. Sometimes when you try to do God's job you screw everything up. And that's exactly what I did, I ended up in jail because I did not let go and let God.

I didn't have any income coming in, because I was doing childcare but I stopped. The Office of Children and Family services interviewed me and afterwards they said I could continue providing childcare services but I didn't. I was depressed and did not feel like it was appropriate for me to provide childcare services under the circumstances.

I searched for jobs over and over again, I went on interviews at least 3 to 4 days out of the week. One time my little daughter said to me, "Mom you don't get discouraged?" I told her if it's not for me, it's not for me. I had just been arrested and I knew it was coming up on the background check because in New York you don't have to be convicted for it to be public record. Once you are arrested it will show up all the time as arrested. Either way it gives an employer a way to discriminate. I was arrested for assault with a deadly weapon, that was not a good look and a red flag for most employers.

One day my old supervisor called me and asked me how I was doing She asked, "What's going on? I've been giving job references for different jobs for you, no one has hired you yet?" I told her no, and I told her about my arrest.

A few days later she called me back and asked me if I would work as a temp. I said, "Yes," and after that I started back working as a receptionist at CT Corporation. During that time, I decided to go back to school to get my bachelors degree. So I was working, going to school and taking care of my daughters.

In 2011 I entered a contest to win tickets to the premiere of 50cent's 2011 movie Things Fall Apart. I forgot what radio station the contest was advertised on but I do remember Angie Martinez and G-Unit being involved with the contest. In order to win the contest you had to send in a video about a time when things have fallen apart for you. Whoever's video was selected was getting tickets to the premiere of Things Fall Apart. I've always liked 50 cent. I've always felt connected to him. I'm a fan of his projects and his intelligence. I joined the contest. I prepared myself to do the video and thought about what I was going to say. I reread the instructions again. Send a video of yourself sharing a time in your life when things fell apart. I started the video off with saying "Sometimes in life things do fall apart but for me things started off apart." I continued with the video and the words naturally flowed out of my mouth as I recorded myself. I gave a timeline and a brief description of my challenges, accomplishments and future goals. I only had to do the video one time, the first time I recorded the video it was perfect. I surprised myself. I won the contest. Right away someone from the G-Unit camp called me up and told me I won the contest. I took my daughters and a friend. When we got to the premiere there was a whole side of seats just for me. Maybe they thought I was going to bring the whole block. The truth is I never rolled like that. I got a chance to see 50 cent. As he walked down the aisle to his seat, he glanced at me. I acted like I didn't see him when he looked my way, but I smiled inside.

I met 50 cent at a club a few days later. I forgot the name of the club but I remember my friend Mumzie and her friend Glenroy worked at the club that night. I met Mumzie from doing childcare. I used to watch her daughter and we became friends. Mumzie knew all the hot spots and all the managers and promoters. Whenever I went out with Mumzie I always had a blast. Mumzie's friend Glenroy was at the door, so it was a piece of cake when it came to getting in the club.

I was sitting at the bar. Probably waiting for a drink. I turned around and 50 cent was right in my face. I didn't know what to say. My friend Mumzie who can be very extroverted, went and told him that I wanted to meet him. I didn't know and he surprised me. He said "Hello," so soft and nice, he caught me off guard. "Are you from London?" he asked. I said no and smiled. We said a few other words to each other, I forget what we said to each other because I was tipsy but I know it was not much. He said nice meeting you and I said nice meeting you. 50 cent walked away and I was so excited I turned around on the bar stool and somehow I fell straight to the floor. I don't think 50 cent saw me. Hopefully he did not see me fall. I will never forget 50 cent and his camp for acknowledging my story.

I'm sharing this story about me winning the contest to say that things started out apart for me and, after Richard got killed, things were bad. I was only 20 years old. My brain was not fully developed, and my mind was still that of a child. I had already had a traumatic life and now I was pushed back down.

FAST FORWARD

Things fall apart, and then things fall back together.

For me things have fallen apart over and over again but they always come back together. One thing I've learned is the timing for things to come back together is all on me.

Richard was a great man, he risked his life in hopes that the generation that came after him, such as his children, would have a different set of circumstances. A support system in a better environment with better choices and more opportunities to grow.

And because he knew the importance of making the right decision when selecting the mother of his children, his legacy will forever live on. That's just the way it goes.

Our daughter, Reshonia, is now an entrepreneur. She is the founder and owner of RichStrands, a brand in honor of her father. She is a project manager and works as a facility coordinator for different companies. Reshonia has been with her fiancé for over 14 years, she met him while she was attending Hofstra University on Long Island. He's from Long Island. Now they have a son together his name is Rich, my first grandchild. Both of my daughters—Reshonia and Gianni both turned out to be smart, productive young ladies. Gianni is my little daughter.

Gianni and Reshonia are seven years apart. Gianni earned her Bachelor's of Science degree from Syracuse University. She was in Syracuse University's IT program. Gianni received full scholarship offers to four different schools. She received an academic scholarship to Syracuse, and that was her dream school, so that's where she decided to go. Gianni is also an entrepreneur. She has a candle company, Ascended Supply, and she also works for one of the top companies in the US. Gianni also loves investing. She's pretty smart when it comes to stocks and stuff like that.

I have so much to be grateful for. I have two amazing daughters, and now I have the smartest grandson, his name is Rich. He is blessed to have a wonderful mother and a wonderful father to take care of him together.

Life has been quite a journey for me so far. I've learned to love, accept, and embrace all of my life experiences, they are special gems. Blessings. Lessons, skills, and knowledge customized to my life, preparing me for the future ahead.

In 2012, I got my Bachelors of Science Degree in Technical Management from Devry University. My concentration was on Business Opps and Human Resource Information Systems. I chose business operations because I always knew I was going to have my own childcare center.

In 2006, I quit my job and started my own family home childcare provider service. My goal was to eventually get a commercial space so I could provide childcare services outside of my home, but I stopped providing servces before I could get an outside space.

In 2012, I started my own fashion brand "amore/Samour." amore/Samour means Love IS Love. Love in Italian and love in French. I created the brand with the hope of spreading love through fashion, jewelry, perfume, cologne and home goods. I worked as a Behavioral Health Specialist on one of NYC's intensive mobile treatment teams, where I provided social and behavior support to some of the city's most vulnerable individuals suffering from homelessness, substance use and mental illness.

I started a petition that can be found on the Change.org website. The petition is to enact a law that would make it mandatory that all children receive therapy as soon as they are removed from their home or placed into the foster care system in NYC.

Currently children are not provided therapy until an extreme behavioral episode happens, then the child is labeled as psychotic and given psychotic medications which they become dependent on them for the rest of their lives. Anytime a child is moved from their parent or a loved one, it is traumatic. It doesn't matter if the removal is just or unjust. It's still a punishment to the child more than a punishment to the adult.

And now I am the author of this book, Richard Porter and I, The Hand Of Circumstance.

Currently I'm single and praying for my husband's protection until we meet. I have to many dreams and I've already started to plant the seeds. One of my biggest dreams is to give others a reason to believe and hope in themselves. Never expect anything from anyone else. Always remember God is not logical, He is magical. Don't ever be scared to dream and believe. If you believe, you will work to achieve your dreams until it becomes a lifestyle full of successes.

Richard was a great man. He was a good father, son, and brother. Richard was more than my daughter's father, he was my companion.

When Richard came into my life, he boosted my confidence. He knocked walls down that had been built up from my past traumatic experiences. I felt safe with Richard. I felt safe to be me.

I'm not saying selling drugs is a good way to come up. However, there are a lot of prominent people that we all look up to today that have changed their circumstances by taking illegal risks.

Richard sacrificed his life, but he knew I would be ok. And when he begged me to have his child over and over again, he was saying he trusted me with his legacy and he was right. And I'm cocky about it.

Post script:

Alberto aka Alpo Martinez was released from prison in 2016 under a witness protection program. It was not long before Alpo found his way back into the lime light. He returned right back to the streets of Harlem with his flashy jewelry, fancy cars, all dressed up in Dior and MCM. He rode up and down the 7th and 8th Avenues on his motorcycle just like old times doing willies and tricks on his bike.

One time I saw him on a social media page laughing and having fun. It made me cry just to know see the person who killed not only my daughter's father but killed so many other fathers, brothers, sons, nephews, grandsons and friends. I never ran into Alpo but a few people from Harlem told me he was hanging out in the bar lounges. They said they kept their distance just in case someone tried to kill him. Well, they were right. It didn't happen right away but on the night of Halloween, October 31, 2021 Alpo Martinez got killed. He got killed in Harlem on 152nd Street on Eighth Avenue, right across from the street from the precinct. According to the news, he was sitting in his vehicle when someone drove up and shot into the car. After getting shot up, it said Alpo attempted to drive himself to Harlem Hospital while throwing narcotics out the window as he was on his way. I don't have anything to say about Alpo getting killed and I don't wish death on anyone. My prayers go out to the families that have been emotionally and mentally affected from his behavior, including himself.

www.ingramcontent.com/pod-product-compliance
Lightning Source LLC
Chambersburg PA
CBHW070924030426
42336CB00014BA/2532